DOSCRIOSTA
(Indestructible)

A Healing Guide for Adult Male
Survivors of Sexual Abuse

Written by:

TaJuan Williams

STOKESMEDIA LLC

TajuanWilliams.com

Doscriostabook.com

1st edition, September 2025

ISBN – 978-1-954851-19-1

Printed in the United States of America

Abstract

"I was not in a relationship with my teacher. I was the victim of a child predator..."

An explosive, powerfully written guide to help adult male survivors of sexual abuse heal themselves. TaJuan Williams selflessly shares both his struggles and successes post victimization with five easy steps to help you to get back to what matters most: your restoration. Williams offers these steps in a motivational fashion and teaches a critical message: ***What happened to you was not your fault.*** And when people seem broken, they can indeed be whole again. Once you take this journey and implement these steps, the roadway to the best version of yourself will be wide open—and you'll be ready to love and appreciate yourself again.

Disclaimer

To protect the privacy of individuals mentioned in this book, some names and identifying details have been changed. Some events are recreated from memory, reflecting my best efforts to portray them truthfully. This book is a reflection of my recollection of events and experiences. While I have strived for accuracy and truthfulness, please understand that memory is subjective and personal interpretation plays a role in recounting past events. Additionally, the opinions expressed in this book are solely mine and do not necessarily reflect the views of any organizations or individuals mentioned. Again, the information presented is based on my personal experiences.

TaJuan Williams

Table of Contents

Foreword

Dr. Carl Stokes Jr. - President and Founder of Stokes Media, LLC

You know how you can have people in your life that you remain bonded with no matter how much time has passed since you last saw them? I can't even describe how elated and honored I was when he reached out to me to be a part of telling his remarkable story. I met TaJuan in my junior year of high school. I came from a private Catholic high school named Turner-Carroll in Buffalo, New York. I did my first two years there and quickly understood that I did not belong. I just didn't fit. I didn't fit in socioeconomically. I didn't fit in socially. I didn't fit in spiritually. I was lonely and miserable. In fact, I was so dejected that after suffering through my freshman and sophomore years there and seeing the financial toll (even with tuition assistance) it was taking on my mother, I decided that I couldn't stomach it anymore. I had no friends. Well, I thought I had friends but gradually found out I didn't. You know how that goes sometimes. Why did it take me two years to decide to move on to a different school if I struggled so much? The answer is quite simple.

At that time, we lived on the west side of the city and the alternative to Turner-Carroll was to attend what was widely deemed as the worst high school in Buffalo. The infamous Grover Cleveland High School was my district school. The school that architecturally resembled the ThunderCats Lair for my Third Earth people who understand. The school that I heard shut down access to the fourth floor due to somebody being thrown out of the window during a brawl. I don't know how true that is, but that was the rumor, and the teachers never gave a straight answer when asked about it. The school where the resources were so limited that the textbooks were literally chained to the desks. What do you mean, homework? How? The school where teachers were actually trafficking drugs. Verified. The school where teachers were openly sleeping with students. Substantiated. Despite all that drama, enrolling at Grover ended up being the best thing to happen to me as I found safety, camaraderie, and finally, a sense of belonging.

Most importantly, Grover Cleveland High School is where I met TaJuan Williams. TaJuan is my brother. It's funny because I don't even remember meeting him. It is as if he was always there. With that being said, it pains me to no end that I was so young and naive that I perceived the relationship he had with one of the teachers at the school as normal, or even cool. The guilt still weighs heavily on me for not recognizing his cries for help. His pleas were disguised through sports, rap music, and our bond of coming from broken, abusive home environments where things that we thought were normal turned out not to be normal at all.

When I think back to how his sexual "conquests" were being presented as if he was some ladies' man who had all the older women after him was really a bunch of child predators passing him around in a not-so-secret human trafficking ring, it hurts me. He wasn't ready for those types of relationships. He just looked the part because he was 6'4, highly intelligent, polite, handsome, and athletic. But TaJuan was just a kid. We both were. Me? I was even less ready for that life than he was. This was evidenced by the two of us being paraded around at his predator's parent's home way out in the suburbs as teens. We were being presented as if we were just some poor, inner-city kids whom she was helping to be successful to "make it out of the hood" despite our circumstances. You know, because we were such good kids, right? Hmmm. I wonder if the two of us being young, attractive, poor, Black inner-city kids with no guidance or familial protection had anything to do with it. It was like the 1990s version of the movie *Get Out*, except the intended use for the bodies was just to satisfy fetishes and fantasies of older White women. It was at that house where I met the teacher's very attractive younger sister. She was an adult also but remember that when you were young, you had no real gauge of how old grown people actually were. A twenty-something year-old is grown as hell to a fifteen-year-old. As I look back on that initial meeting out in charming, New York, I now realize that I may have been intended to be a possible romantic option for the younger sister orchestrated by the older sister who already had her sharp talons dug deep into TaJuan. Due to association, I was able to be hand delivered as another fresh, virile, and most importantly, unprotected option. It was all set up like a sadistic "two-man" way before social media was a thing. However, I was too green and inexperienced to understand what was happening. That, along with being completely overwhelmed with being at a house of that magnitude with these rich White people. I mean, it was an immaculate home with furniture, countless rooms and decor as if it was staged for a magazine shoot. I had never seen anything like that before then. Their normal life was a life goal for me. A beautiful home in a nice, quiet neighborhood with a yard, matching furniture, and a refrigerator full of food. I didn't truly understand disparity until that day. With all of that going on, I was way too mesmerized by the atmosphere to recognize what the situation really was.

It was so deep that we were invited to join a bar-sponsored softball league with TaJuan and I the only teenagers there. In fact, we were the only Black people there. After each game, we would all be at the bar that sponsored the team on Chippewa Street in downtown Buffalo. Research suggests that Black youth are often perceived as older in a phenomenon called adultification. Seeing us as older could maybe justify some of the interactions that took place. That may have been the case for random bar patrons as it pertained to us, but the desperate housewives that were all over us knew damn well how old we were. TaJuan ended up sleeping with several other women in the league and around the bar. It was literally a running joke with some of the adults in the circle. They were basically taking turns with him.

Unfortunately, during this time my man was drinking…a lot. Many times, after the games, I stayed at the bar and suffered through the awkwardness and discomfort because I was so worried about him. I personally could not stand a sloppy, drunk ass woman with her eyes half closed, all up in my personal space in an obnoxiously loud bar, yelling about some nonsense I can't even understand while blowing that disgusting alcohol breath in my face. Repulsive. We were underage and shouldn't even have been there in the first place. TaJuan's drinking became too regular, too frequent, and his tolerance to alcohol and sexual misconduct became far too high. The dude was numb. As this pattern persisted it soon became pointless for me to continue hanging around at the bar because ultimately some grown White lady would always make sure that he got home "safely."

Eventually it all became too much for me, and it impacted our friendship significantly. Not that there was any sort of falling out between us; I just found myself losing someone I cared about so much to a life that I was not mentally or emotionally prepared to deal with. I also didn't know how to articulate what I was feeling at the time. How do you tell your boy at sixteen years old that you are worried that he is getting free drinks and unlimited sex from a bunch of older women? At that age, where I come from, you don't.

To this day, I have never had a drink. Other than the wine at communion during my Catholic church days and my late father, Carl Stokes Sr. letting me sip his 40oz of Colt 45 when I was a kid, I don't even know what alcohol tastes like. I've seen it destroy too much. I watched it hurt my best friend and dim his bright light. I'm not going to tell too much of the story because it is not my story to tell. What I will say is that it is a unique approach to this topic, especially from the male perspective. It expresses the complexities in race, sex, class and age when manipulation and exploitation take place in its most calculated form. Nonetheless, seeing my man make this incredible journey and find himself again is one of the best things I have seen happen. It is one of the best things I could have hoped for. Additionally, being the person he is, he has decided to share his journey of healing with others who need healing themselves…even though he suffered through his own pain in private for many, many years.

Ladies and gentlemen, I proudly present to you, *Doscriosta (Indestructible): A Healing Guide for Adult Male Survivors of Sexual Abuse* by TaJuan Williams.

Introduction

The first thing I get asked is, "TJ, what is with the weird book title?!" Fair question. The explanation goes as follows: It took me forty-plus years to realize that I was indestructible. To determine one's indestructibility, he must have had numerous accounts of situations in life that could have destroyed him. My guess is that you are reading this book because you can relate. Now, between songs, movies, books and other media, the title, *Indestructible* has been utilized repeatedly. I get why that is. The word resonates with many people through various situations whether in fact or fiction. That word definitely describes me as I stand before you as a completely healed man today. However, for the purpose of this book my take on the word has been translated into the Celtic language of Gaelic – Doscriosta (dosh-kris-tah). No, I am not of Scottish or Irish descent, but the person who took advantage of me as a minor and had me put in jail as a young adult is.

Let's start from the middle. Me shackled up at twenty-two years old and being told in court by an Erie County sheriff, "I bet you weren't complaining then," has replayed in my head over and over throughout the years. You see? This type of thought process just highlights the double standard of sexual behavior and/or expectations of sexual behavior between men and women. This double standard praises boys and men for hyperactive heterosexual sexual activity, while girls and women are heavily stigmatized for similar behaviors. Now, when it comes to child predators, society often villainizes (and rightfully so) the perpetrators when girls are the victims. Us men don't get that same consideration or protection because the general consensus is simply that males want sex, especially teenage males. This is, of course, assuming that the boy is not a small child.

This is so evident that you can watch a series of comedy sketches on *Saturday Night Live* featuring Pete Davidson as he portrays a high school kid who has sex with his "hot teacher." The skit highlights numerous positives of a teenage boy having sex with an attractive female teacher. For example, the kid's father and grandfather go from being estranged to close again due to bonding over the boy's perceived accomplishment. Or the kid being an absolute hero amongst his peers at school being affectionately called things like, *The Chosen One, King of Everything,* or the punchline joke, *My Man...* but like the way Denzel Washington says it.

SNL also had a skit where a lonely female teacher portrayed by the very funny Tina Fey was obsessed with her male student being played by a young Justin Bieber as she fantasizes about him serenading her. The skit presents the teacher's inner monologue out loud where she mentions that the young boy's smile is, "like watching a baby bunny sniffing a flower" while the camera pans over to the pop star's precocious grin before he breaks into a song. The inner monologue proceeds to mention how she doesn't know whether she wants to marry him or push around the mall in a stroller, suggesting a comedic take on the Jocasta complex. In Greek mythology, Jocasta is the mother of Oedipus, who killed his father and married his mother. This story became the basis of the phallic stage in Sigmund Freud's psychosexual stages of development.

Poor kid. Between skits like that and being publicly swooned over and groped by countless celebrity women (and men) at award shows, interviews and events, you can see the exhaustion in a now adult Justin Bieber's eyes. You can see the toll that being regarded as a plaything by adults has taken on him over the years. Hell, Adam Sandler's whole movie, *That's My Boy* is a comedy about a kid fathering a child with a hot teacher and living a perceived male child's fantasy. Interesting how these same people would go ballistic if it was some "creepy" male taking advantage of a female child. Like I said before, double standard.

For me, experiencing that court officer victim blaming me for being taken advantage of at a young age cut me deeply. In fact, when it came to that hurtful statement of, "I bet you weren't complaining then," I didn't even have time to process. Before I could even react, I saw that my own lawyer was laughing with him in agreement. I immediately saw what side they were on. They were on the side of society that believed that a young male being victimized in an inappropriate, emotionally toxic and manipulative relationship could not actually be a victim if he was getting sex out of it. So, yes. Maybe I didn't complain about it at the time. Maybe I was too immature to know there were grounds for complaints. Perhaps I had no one to complain to. Maybe I did tell people, but it just fell on deaf ears. I mean, just about every adult in my life had their own issues to the point where I was more so looking after them. My mother was certainly in no position to do anything. My friends all thought it was normal because of the environment we came from. Hell, I thought it was normal because I was from the same environment. I actually lost my virginity at twelve years old to a prostitute named Cassidy that used to live with us. My parents used to smoke crack for days on end and there were always tons of people in and out of the house. I learned how to drink, roll blunts, play poker and have sex all before I got to the seventh grade.

More importantly, maybe I didn't tell anyone because like many victims, I cared about my abuser. There was no way I would risk getting her into any trouble. Unfortunately, I was misled into thinking that she also cared about me. You know, really cared outside of the fetish for young, impoverished, Black male youth. Hell of a savior complex, huh? Imagine your teacher with whom you were in a secret relationship, being upset with you when you showed interest in an age-appropriate girl. Or better yet, disliking teenage girls for naturally having interest in you as an age-appropriate boy. That was the case for me. I was in deep. I just didn't know how deep until I graduated high school and thought we could finally be exclusive. You know, in an actual mature relationship where I didn't have to be hidden like an embarrassment or some dark secret that could take down an empire if exposed. That's when I found out that I was just being used as nothing more than a temporary plaything.

I waited patiently, yet excitedly to graduate high school so I could openly be with someone I thought loved me. It turns out that I was waiting the same way a side piece waits for their person to break up with their actual significant other in hopes that they would finally be together officially. In other words, it was never going to happen but only one of us knew this. Instead, I was made to look like an obsessed, violent stalker when all I wanted was answers as to why. That search for answers got me locked up in the Erie County Holding Center where I was beaten, left naked for days and constantly being threatened by sheriff's deputies at the requests of my abuser's connected relatives and friends. Imagine being humiliated by law enforcement during their effort to protect a criminal. I guess a criminal is only a criminal if people respect the victim. There I was, another Black man who was an actual victim of the pseudo-victimization, phony fear, and crocodile tears of a White woman. Well, I guess that is what people can pull off when they come from a prominent family with political ties in Western New York.

STEP ONE

Acknowledge

"You can't heal what you don't reveal."
Sean (Jay-Z) Carter

The first step to healing is to *Acknowledge*. This is because I had to learn a very important fact about my upbringing and that fact is pretty straightforward. Simply put, it wasn't my fault, just like what happened to you was not your fault. You must acknowledge the fact that you were a child and that you did not choose your circumstances or any of the events that followed. You are not responsible for the events that took place. They were a byproduct of the situation you were born into and the circumstances you were given. We get dealt the hands we were meant to play the game of life with, and we make the best of those cards.

You will see throughout this book that there are several adults, family members, and would be mandated reporters that will fail me. You probably had many adults fail you as well. We are not the failures of those individuals. I say that because as victims we too often take ownership of the follies of our journey while trying to navigate through the pain and trauma without a compass. We blame ourselves for the misguided paths we have often taken into adulthood. Acknowledge that you were victimized. I know that "victim" sounds like a swear word nowadays, especially coming from a Black person, but you are. This is not the same as having a victim mindset. That is when a person sees themselves as always being wronged no matter the situation. This is different. Sometimes a cookie is just a cookie. Do you understand? What I mean is that some things are what they are, objectively. You being taken advantage of during a vulnerable age and/or time in your life is exactly what it is. I remember referring to my time with my abuser as a relationship and a good friend had to remind me that what I was in was not a relationship, I was the victim of a predator. Think about your situation and see if you can relate.

The most difficult part of telling any story is where to begin. I know it's easy to say "just start from the beginning." However, the beginning of this tale originates similarly to most traumas, somewhere long before I came into the world. I guess in my case the beginning would start with a petite southern Black woman named Naomi.

Naomi, or the woman I would grow to call Grandma, was born in Macon, Georgia. Although I don't know her entire story it had been speculated that she fled the south due to suspicion of murder and ended up settling on the east side of Buffalo, NY in the early 1950s. After an initial marriage and divorce she would give birth to and subsequently groom the monster that would grow up to become my father. I wish I knew what caused my grandmother so much pain in her life that she drank every day, all day for sixty-plus years. Better yet, I'm curious to know what events took place that led her to be a foul-mouthed, abusive, sadistic, and cruel woman. Even though Naomi moved in that rough direction, I know for a fact she loved me and to be perfectly honest, she was always proud of me. I feel a bit conflicted about portraying her in this manner, but it is the truth. A person can be more than one thing in life and their impact can vary from encounter to encounter. King Leopold II of Belgium probably killed eight figures worth of African people and still possessed the ability to be kind to the people he cared about.

The doting, smiling, gentle woman that I knew as a grandson was nothing like that to her actual children or the men who loved her throughout the years. Even my own scattered memories of her reflect those dualities. As this story progresses, hopefully you can understand the complicated emotions I have in dealing with all the adults that were present in my life. I learned a long time ago that nothing is ever as simple as we are led to believe. I guess there is always some good in even the worst of us. One person's John Wayne Gacy is another person's Ned Flanders!

Nobody, and I mean nobody, could string together a series of swear words like my grandmother. Contrarily, no woman in the world was more of a sophisticated lady than she was. Her style, hair, and jewelry were always on point. The way she held and smoked her Virginia Slims often reminded me of a silver screen 1950s actress or a jazz singer on stage in a fancy night club back in her era. She loved her rum, her parties, and her public image. Behind closed doors, she was an abusive tyrant that ruled with pure fear and violence.

Naomi, through her series of encounters and two marriages, gave birth to four children, all of whom would grow up to inflict their own traumas upon their children. No one more so than her oldest and largest son, my father Tony. I only know a few details of the relationship between Naomi and Tony and none of them are good. When you ask my aunts and uncles, they will tell you that all the abuse that was inflicted upon him by their mother was transferred directly to them as siblings. My father didn't talk much about his mother and how she raised him but sometimes he would speak of the horror show and provide some insight into what may have led to him becoming the man that he became. The man that would grow up to continue the family cycle of inflicting pain upon the next generation. I have always viewed my grandmother as the epicenter of it all but that may be unfair since I know so very little about what she experienced during her upbringing. Like I said in the opening, "Who really knows where the trauma started?" I am merely another link in the chain of family abuse. I don't want to absolve my father of any wrongdoing by discussing his mother; I just want to provide a backdrop for the events that were to come.

My grandfather was a tall, slender and deep voiced man named William. There is much speculation as to whether he is in fact my biological grandfather, but nonetheless, he is the only grandfather that I had ever known. I will tell you though, from what I remember of him, William was a good man. It didn't occur to me until I became a teenager that there had to be some serious issues in their marriage since I never saw them show any sort of affection towards one another. They even slept in separate bedrooms. I have some very fond memories of my grandfather. That man loved cookouts and knew how to throw a party! I remember one summer for a backyard barbeque William bought a brand new 20-gallon trash can and half-dozen containers of Kool-Aid and filled it with a water hose. We were "kid drunk" for days! William was the one person that I can remember that could tune Naomi out and keep moving as cool as a cucumber. I remember the day that he died. It was like a light went out in that house that never switched back on.

The details of the abuse that transpired in my father's childhood are the subject of much speculation. Neither my father nor his siblings ever really spoke much about what actually happened to them growing up. However, the evidence of trauma permeated through the walls of the house on Goulding Avenue. Some of the stories included beatings, my father being burned on a stove intentionally, lots of verbal abuse and even sexual abuse. The alcoholism involved, though? That was the key to it all. As far as I can remember, the smell of rum and Virginia Slims dominated that house. I am sure there are tons of other things that I cannot recall from those days. I was just a child and wasn't privy to the particulars related to my father and grandmother's relationship, but I can assure you it was begrudged love at best. Even after all of that, my grandmother was always proud of me for some reason, and I know she loved me. I can think of plenty of times when she bragged about my accomplishments. She even paid for my trip to Italy in the 8th grade when I attended school #38. The one thing I did learn from my grandmother is that a person can mean totally different things to different people. To me she was sweet, always smiling and proud. To others she was mean, abusive, and nasty. Enough about her now. I just wanted to set a foundation for you in hopes that you can look into your family history to determine if somewhere down the line the tone was set for what you ended up experiencing.

Now, let's get down to what this story is about.

I know there are tons of abuse survivors in this world and their stories are filled with unimaginable horrors. This story also has some of those elements. Some of them were mine directly, and some are events that I witnessed and honestly, even inflicted on others by me. I hope this story can provide hope for you. I intend to provide a quantum of solace for anyone out there that feels that sense of dread and hopelessness and express that there can be great adventure and love for you in life. I also intend to provide empathy, understanding, and relatability for you survivors who have already worked through those feelings of hopelessness. I am with you. I am you.

I have often compared my early life to an alien being born on a planet like Neptune. Imagine what it would be like to be born and raised on a planet with 1200 mph winds and raging storms daily, then suddenly one day you are transplanted here to Earth, and the sun is shining, the winds are gentle and even at its worst it is nothing compared to the place from which you came. My problem in life wasn't learning how to weather a storm; it was learning how to live in the peace of the sunshine.

I was raised on the East side of Buffalo, NY in the 1980s when the violence of the streets was in its infancy. We lived in a single-family home in a predominantly Black neighborhood on the corners of Woodlawn Avenue and Wohlers Avenue, right over by school #53. My Buffalo people know exactly where I'm talking about. For my people outside of Buffalo, school #53 is about two minutes away from the unprovoked, racially motivated sneak attack on Black people at the Jefferson Avenue Tops Market that took place on May 14, 2022.

My parents had been married for about five years prior to my birth, and it would be another five before they would have their 6th child. I am the oldest son and the middle child. (Yes, I have middle child syndrome!) My two older sisters, Chontra and Anika, were the ones who cared for me the most and I credit them with the bulk of my upbringing. They were my rocks. Despite suffering repeated physical and sexual abuse from the man who was supposed to protect them, they still found the compassion, time, and love to not only raise their siblings but their own children and now grandchildren. The details of those abuses were unfortunately buried with him when he passed away. I wish he had to face the public shaming he deserved for his crimes against them. The physical and emotional scars that monster left behind did not close for me until I gave his eulogy. I hope they found some peace that day too. They are two of the strongest women this world has ever produced, and I am eternally grateful for them. I have five siblings in total. After my two older sisters, there are me and the three younger siblings who were always clustered into the essence of one single entity affectionately called "Y'all Four." Thankfully, my youngest brother Tony did not suffer as much direct abuse, and my little sister Andrea was spared the rampant sexual abuse from my father. My brother, Adrian, and I endured constant physical and mental abuse from him that would later shape all of our insecurities. Unfortunately, it is not that rare for a home to be riddled with the number of abuses we suffered and in turn normalized. The extent to which those abuses were carried out and the cold-hearted way in which my parents operated is a psychiatrist's dream. As I said, Tony Williams was the single most abusive human being I have ever known. No one was spared and no one was safe from him or with him. I haven't mentioned my mother much, but she will be the subject of lots of conversation throughout this story. I will spare you all the details for now and maybe address them in another book for another time. I will pick up this story after the crack parties, strangers living in our home, and stints at homeless shelters. I am going to skim past the years of physical and sexual violence, the constant verbal and emotional abuse and get to the matter at hand. How does one become ripe for a predator? Easy. You are failed by EVERY adult around you.

When I was fifteen years old, we lived in a small three-bedroom apartment on a street ironically named Normal Avenue, a place that was far from it. My older sisters had children by then and were nineteen and twenty years old, respectively. See, back then in many Black households, we were raised to believe that by the time you turned eighteen you were considered grown and had to move out of the home. Coincidentally, this was the same age that my mother was no longer able to receive welfare benefits for us. I remember when my mother came into the room, wreaking of body odor as usual. (We had nicknamed her "Stank.") While my father slept, she asked me to assist her in escaping as she would often do. She wanted to leave to get help. She told me that she was going to get clean and that she would be back for us. So, at 5:15am on May 15, 1994, I grabbed my mother's clothes that she had hidden in a trash bag, carried them to the curb and left them outside as if I were taking out the trash. She would later sneak out, grab her belongings and head to rehab. I wouldn't live with my mother again for another two years after that. After she left, she would spend the next twenty-eight days in a rehab in upstate NY. During her absence a lot of things changed in that home. Most noticeably, my father's abusive behavior worsened. However, the strength and toughness of myself and my siblings grew, culminating in the fight for our life as we called it.

One summer day, I returned from hanging out at what would become my safe haven over the years, my friends Russell and Jason's house on 14th Street. I had not yet met Carl and Damon. There was no "Bomb S.Q.U.A.D." yet. That crew formed later when the five of us all became tight. S.Q.U.A.D. stood for Skills Qualified Unlimited and Deadly, referring to our rap talents and overall cohesiveness. Before all of that took place, there were only me, Russ, and Jay as young men sitting on a porch telling stories and laughing at the world.

When I had arrived home that evening I forgot to close the back door all the way and of course any minor infraction was met with swift and brutal assault from my father. As I sat on the sofa attempting to watch the tiny 20-inch television we had in the living room, he suddenly and viciously punched me dead in the face. As I tried to re-gather my senses, I saw my little brother Adrian leap from the other sofa and began to attempt to place him in a choke hold. Me, fearing for Adrian's life, reached back with all the strength I could muster and hit him in the face as hard as I could, knocking his ass right off his feet—man, that still feels good to this day! He fell to the ground, and we hit him with everything we had that night. We got busy until we tired ourselves out. Towards the end, he nonchalantly asked, "Are y'all finished?" and stood up and walked away as if nothing had happened. Oh, did I forget to mention that my father stood 6'6" and weighed close to 300 pounds? I'm not talking about the soft and fluffy kind of 300 pounds, either. I am talking about 300 pounds of straight granite. He was the most physically powerful human I have ever witnessed. He let us beat him up that day and I still have no idea why. After that we lived in absolute fear, taking shifts sleeping with knives and locking all doors. That went on until my mother called one day and said she was going to call the police to get him out of the house. I was not there, but I was told that when they arrived my father was in his room with a prostitute getting high, and he was promptly taken into custody. When I got home, my mother arrived to say that she would be back later. However, we did not see her again for another year. My older sisters, Chontra and Anika, had moved out on their own by then, so Andrea, Adrian, Tony, and I, ages 10–15, also known as "Y'all Four" had become "Us Four," and we had no choice but to figure it out on our own. The summer to pass that year was filled with four children and then eventually one of their slightly older teenage sisters trying to find our way through life. We did what we needed to do to eat, keep the lights on, and the roof over our heads. I will spare the details of those events in this story.

I began my sophomore year at Grover Cleveland High school as a completely different kid. I was taller, more worldly, and a hell of a lot more fearless. I had in fact become a bit of a bully and a foul-mouthed hooligan earning the nickname "TaJuan Tourette's" for my instant fly off the handle verbal assaults on anyone that slightly crossed me. I was angry all the time and I resented anyone that had stability in their lives. Mostly though, my anger was taken out on my teachers. Especially a geometry teacher named Ms. Darren, a portly redhead who was, by all means, a good teacher who recognized my ability to comprehend the materials and solve equations. She tried to push me, but in those days all I did was push back until I was effectively banned from her classroom and failed for the year. Although I was kicked out of class, I was permitted to attend a study hall in that very same room. During 7th period one day in March of 1995, there I would then meet the person who would introduce me to a type of abuse I was unfamiliar with. In the class stood a young, wild-haired, and obviously hungover teacher who would take over monitoring that study hall. For the purposes of anonymity, I will refer to her as "Breanne," as in the Gaelic word "bréan," which means foul. From the moment I met Breanne, my life would never be the same.

You would probably think that this was a story of love at first sight, or some pleasant interaction between the two of us that would spark some conversation that led to the events that would unfold. That could not be further from the truth. In fact, our first conversation would not happen for a few weeks into her new role as the study hall teacher. The first time she ever even acknowledged me was when she overheard me speaking Italian to another student named Giovanni who was one of many international students in that school. Grover Cleveland had housed many students from all over the globe and Giovanni was a lonely kid who barely spoke a word of English. So, I would spend my study hall time talking to Gio and it sharpened my skills. As I was leaving that day, she stopped me in the doorway and asked where I learned how to speak Italian. I told her about my time at school #38 and our trip to Italy. She was impressed, remarking that it took a special kind of mind to be able to speak another language so well at such a young age.

Interestingly, the following day that tone would change. As the study hall started, I had blood on my mind. There was another student named Julius who owed me money and I was going to get my money back that day one way or another. I approached him and asked for the money. The usual excuses began and "TaJuan Tourette's" emerged. The chain of swear words and threats would have made Samuel L. Jackson blush! That is when I felt a hand on my arm, and I turned to swing. It was Breanne. I paused but did not stop my tirade and I had in fact focused it on her. She promptly called for security, and I was once again removed from Ms. Darren's classroom. Later that same day I felt terrible for some reason. I went home and made a lemon bundt cake (yes, this is true) and wrapped it up. The following day I handed the cake to Breanne and apologized for the outburst. She asked me to step into the hallway and told me to never act like that again. She told me that I was better than that and she could clearly see that I was "different" from everyone around me. "You don't belong here; there is a lot about you that I can see that maybe you don't," were the words she used. After that, we would begin to talk regularly, and I would always look forward to study hall.

We would sit at her desk and talk for the entire hour. I learned about her role at the school. She was a teacher for a special program that catered to kids who were on the verge of dropping out. She and the other teachers in the program were young and were all friends. She was twenty-four years old, basically fresh out of college and really loved teaching. She would ask me about my home life, friends, and interests. We talked about her father, who was her idol, and her brother and his ambitions to become a judge or an FBI agent. Other than family stuff, we mostly talked about her drinking. Breanne loved to drink. It was almost stereotypical how this young Irish girl loved to be at the bar "getting hammered" as she put it so often.

Grooming

I would turn sixteen that year and, on my birthday, I arrived at the study hall where I was welcomed with a cake and a gift brought to me by none other than Breanne. I remember it like it was yesterday. It was a beautiful chocolate cake with red Swedish fish on top. She learned about my sweet tooth from early on. It was the kindest, most thoughtful thing anyone had ever done for me at that point in my life. Unfortunately, I did not understand the concept of grooming back then. Grooming behavior in sex offenders is an extremely calculated process that is used to manipulate and exploit people in order to gain their trust and ultimately abuse them. Think about a predator seeing a young child in the neighborhood after watching him or her for weeks. The predator notices that the child is often alone and knows that they don't have a strong family support system. The predator will strategically start with small talk.

Predator: "Hey there little guy! Do you remember me? I live down the street from you. How are you today?"

Child: "Fine."

Predator: "Okay, I will catch you around. Oh, by the way, I like your Marvel t-shirt!"

Child: Smiles and says, "Thanks!"

A few days later the predator sees the kid again.

Predator: "Hello again little guy! I was hoping to run into you. I have been carrying around these cool socks with Marvel characters on them. I saw them at the store and thought you would like them."

The child appears to be a bit skeptical, but the socks are really cool. The predator notices the child's hesitation, so he purposely hands the kid the socks while distracting him with a question, so the exchange takes place without further hesitation.

Predator: "Who is your favorite Marvel character?"

Child: "Black Panther is my favorite."

Predator: "No way! Mine too. Is he on the socks?"

Child: Takes a look and socks and says, "Yes!"

Predator: "Well, I'm glad you like them. Okay, I have to run. I will see you around!"

Another few days go by. Predator sees the kid walking home from school by himself.

Predator: "Hey...there's my guy! How are those socks working out for you?"

Child: "Great! All my friends think they are so cool!"

Predator: "You know what? I actually have a friend who works at Marvel. He just gave me a whole bunch of Black Panther stuff. There's Black Panther toys, clothes, and even rare comics! It is too much stuff for me! Maybe you would like some of it. It's right down the street in my house. You want to come in and take a look?!"

That's one way grooming behavior sneaks up on unsuspecting victims. It's a cold world.

Grooming is a method used by perpetrators to lower a victim's resistance, minimize the risk of being discovered, and maintain control. Now, in my case I can see that my predator had me in her sights well before that cake was even baked. You see, that's how it begins. It could be something as seemingly insignificant as a baked good. None of the other kids got a cake. They all had birthdays too, right? Some of them came from homes just as broken as mine and needed guidance as well. Some were also incredibly smart. But still...no cakes. That's how they do it. They make you feel special. You feel chosen and above the fray. It always starts small. A cupcake, a compliment, a private conversation. Then come the privileges. A little extra access, more attention, fewer rules, better treatment and so on. Was I a vulnerable target? Absolutely. Looking at it symbolically, the Swedish fish on top of the cake was profound. I was like a fish on the hook and that cake was the bait that lured me in for the catch. I never stood a chance, and she knew it.

As I got to know Breanne and the other teachers in the program, I also met another young man named Alonzo. Like me, he came from a home that was fractured and uncertain. He too was hungry for guidance and for mentorship. Like me, he sought some kind of steady light in the dark world around him. Breanne had taken an interest in Alonzo's well-being and even though I can't prove it, I believe that he may have been her first inappropriate target or at the least, the student she first began testing boundaries with. That is something else you need to acknowledge. You may not have been the first, last, or only victim of your abuser.

Over time Breanne's concern for me deepened, or at least that's how it felt. She asked about my family, my feelings and my struggles. I'm not going to lie, she made me feel seen. I felt needed and protected. On the last day of school that year, she handed me a torn piece of notebook paper. Her address and phone number were written in neat cursive. It was presented with the kind of effort you only see from someone who wants to be remembered. "Call me if you ever need anything," she said, looking directly into my eyes. I remember wanting to call her at that very moment. I felt so safe with her. I felt special and comforted. I knew she could help me. I could even sense the attraction, though I wasn't sure what that meant or what to do with it. I still remember that phone number. I still remember the color of the paper and the exact way it was torn from the spiral binding. I did call her that summer, more than once. Unfortunately, it would never reach her until one day a man answered. He said he'd take a message and get it to her. That summer would be my last normal teenage summer.

Surviving

Despite everything, my siblings and I were managing to survive. We lived alone but started having semi-regular contact with our mother again. She had a new boyfriend named Weldon, a man she'd met in rehab. They lived together in the Lake View Projects on the west side, along with Weldon's mother. Weldon was kind to us. A gentle soul. He didn't have to, but he showed up and treated us like we mattered. In a world of people who wanted something from you, he just gave. Weldon would play a significant role in this story too but more on that later. Rest in peace, sir, and thank you.

Anyway, we needed an adult around. I called my mother once to ask her for food. The refrigerator was broken, and we were starving. She arrived that afternoon with a half loaf of bread and a can of tuna fish. She then had to immediately leave because she had to return to the cookout at Weldon's mother's house. Imagine that. A mother with her four hungry children at home and bringing them scraps so she could hurry to return to her feast. That was all we needed to know and confirmed we were in fact on our own for real. I ended up connecting with a friend of one of my sisters named "G." He was a good guy who was really into some bad things and hooked me up with the opportunity to make a little side money. G showed me the first cell phone I had ever seen in person. Back then to have a phone like that meant that you had some serious cash and he put me onto the street game. I did a variety of activities for money whether it was dropping off packages (which I never opened) or delivering guns to people for what he called, "one time use." I wasn't always a willing participant in these types of activities, but it paid the bills, and I had plenty of cash to make sure we had food and clothes. That is how we survived during that time.

That fall, I started my junior year of high school with a renewed sense of self. I trained hard over the summer and earned my place as the starting quarterback on the varsity football team. For once, things seemed to be aligning. I was excited, focused, and hopeful. Breanne found me right away on the first day back. We walked through the halls of Grover Cleveland, catching up on our summers. She apologized, explaining she hadn't been home over the break. She stayed with her parents. The man who answered the phone that time was her brother, who'd been staying at her place. I told her how excited I was to be playing football that year. She lit up and said she'd be coming to my games.

Just hearing that sent a feeling of thrill right through me. I never had someone in the stands cheering for me personally. The thought gave me butterflies. I wanted to impress her, though I didn't really understand why. Her excitement felt real, too. So real that for a moment I let myself believe it was only excitement for the sport and nothing more.

Then came the first game of the season. With the whole school watching, I played the absolute worst game of my life! Not just bad. It was disastrous. I threw four, maybe five interceptions. Each mistake wasn't just a brick; it was a weight that dragged me further under. By the fourth turnover, I wasn't playing football anymore. I don't know what the hell I was doing out there other than obviously drowning in front of everyone. I walked over to the bench, sat down, and buried my head in my hands. I remember wishing that I could just fold into myself and vanish. I don't know if it was the pressure or if deep down, I was carrying too many invisible weights and expectations. I didn't understand. I had wounds I hadn't yet identified. That game marked the beginning of a shift in my life. It was a realization that I wasn't just fighting for yardage under Friday night lights. I was surviving on a field where no one else could see the stakes were life itself. On the bus ride home after the game I sat in my seat silently. My teammates would console me, and my coach would give me the usual pep talk that all coaches give. None of it resonated, mattered or impacted me in any real way.

I went home and could barely sleep thinking about the embarrassing performance I had just put on.

The next morning while walking in the hallway at school I felt a gentle touch across my arm. I turned around and there she was. She told me that she was at the game and that she was not disappointed in my performance. What she was disappointed in was the fact that I had my head hanging and looked defeated. She said, "I don't ever want to see you hang your head like that again." I promised that I would be better. Before that moment I did not have a standard in which to live by. This was the turning point for us. Soon, we would be walking and talking in the hallways daily.

In October of that year, my mother returned to our lives and my brothers, and I moved into her apartment in a different part of the west side. The building looked half-condemned, but hey…it had a roof, and it was warm. Weldon had moved in with her too, and all of us shared that cramped three-bedroom apartment. Weldon was unemployed. My mother had found a job working as a factory packager, but her salary wasn't enough to support us all. I was no longer running the streets or making money illegally, which meant things were even tighter than before.

Breanne's Apartment

One day, though, my mother gave me money for a haircut which was a rare treat back then. My sister's boyfriend recommended a shop across town, but I didn't have a way to get there. The next day at school, I mentioned that to Breanne. She enthusiastically offered to take me after school. I was elated. That afternoon we got into her vehicle. This was a place where I would eventually spend a lot of time and would become the scene of many carnal and criminal encounters. As we drove to the barbershop, we talked about my family. Specifically, we talked about my siblings and my mother. At the time, I thought she was just genuinely interested. Now, I understand it differently. Those conversations were more than casual. They were probing for opportunities and confirming my vulnerabilities. Another thing I must keep reminding myself of is that *I was a child*. No matter how big I was or how mature I thought I'd become, I was still a child. There was nothing normal about this interaction or the ones that would follow.

When we arrived at the barbershop, I asked if she wanted to come inside. She said she would stay in the car and catch up on grading assignments. I'll never forget that haircut. It took over an hour but when it was done, I had the design I wanted. The Carolina Panthers logo shaved into the back of my head. The whole time I was in the chair I couldn't help but laugh to myself. The barber and the other patrons kept looking suspiciously at her sitting outside alone in her car. They thought she was a cop, and in that neighborhood, at that time of night, that was probably a good thing for her safety. Afterwards, she asked if I was hungry. Of course I was! I was a teenage boy. We stopped at a pizzeria near her place, grabbed a box and that was when we went to her apartment together for the first time. Just like the vehicle, this would be another place where I would spend a lot of time.

I still remember the smell of that little converted attic apartment. The tiny stove. The view from the back windows. The bathroom that was just off the kitchen. I can close my eyes right now and see it all. The recliner and bookshelf, the chair in the corner by the phone, the nook by the fire escape where her dining table sat, and most of all that bedroom. It contained the most comfortable bed I had ever laid in up to that point in my life. The sound of Sarah McLachlan singing graced the atmosphere. We sat there for an hour or so talking about everything from food to family to life in general. Then the conversation turned to music. She asked who I liked. I pulled the *Bone Thugs-N-Harmony, E. 1999 Eternal* CD out of my bag and played a song called *"Mo Murda."* That was my favorite song on the album, and she loved it too, which made me feel even closer to her.

She sat on the sofa, let her hair down, and bopped her head to the beat. I watched her and at the time, I didn't realize this was another step in the grooming process. She was feigning interest and mirroring me. That's another thing that predators do. They like what you like. They want what you want. They erase or overshadow the differences between themselves and you. In this case she erased or overshadowed the differences between a 25-year-old woman and a 16-year-old boy. "See how much we have in common?" she said jovially. After we finished the song, she drove me home. Days after that she called me with another invitation, taking another step forward to normalizing us together alone at her place.

I had a friend before my Bomb S.Q.U.A.D. days. Jacob was my football teammate. He was an average height, wiry strong, and passionate kid that would first teach me how to rap. Jacob and I never really agreed on much and those constant disagreements led to our eventual falling out as friends as we steadily took divergent paths throughout the school year. However, during the time I first started getting to know Breanne, he was my closest friend. Breanne called me and asked if I wanted to bring a friend over for a movie night. I asked Jacob if he wanted to come with me and he agreed. Breanne also had a friend with her that night, a woman named Stacy. We walked over to her house and arrived to see the very inviting presentation of snacks. She had popcorn, soda and an arrangement of different types of candy laid out just for us. She put on the movie *Animal House*, which now that I think about it, was a pretty explicit movie. So, there we sat, Stacy on the loveseat and me on the sofa with Breanne sitting between me and Jacob.

For those who never saw it, *Animal House* is filled with sex, laughs, drugs, and nudity, something I would later learn are tools to lower a victim's apprehensions about these subjects to again normalize the abnormal. Stacy would later joke to Breanne that they just had a "double date" with a couple of high school guys. As I think back on it, that night was not just for me. It was to regularize Breanne and I being together for our friends. A couple of days later we would have another movie night. This one was more erotic and passionate than the one before as we watched a movie with Brad Pitt called *Legends of the Fall*. It was an intense romantic film about a man who was in love with his brother's wife. Again, another movie loaded with adult themes and sex. This was followed by another very adult movie starring Harrison Ford called *Presumed Innocent*, which was again loaded with sex and adult themes.

That night was the first night we really touched. As we would sit there and watch these movies, I would rub her hands. (She had told me how much she loved hand rubs, especially the individual fingers). Every moment steadily became more and more intimate. I can still see the shadows of the candlelight dancing off the walls and their lilac scent in the air. I remember the coffee table and position of the tv angled in the corner of the room as we sat on the couch watching movies in silence.

Two days after her birthday, we would again convene in her apartment. The soft candle lit living room awaited me as I arrived, and we sat down to watch the movie, *Ghost*. I have not watched that movie since, and the mere mention of it still makes my skin crawl. My sister is also a survivor of sexual abuse. When we talk about the subject, she often describes the background of what was happening. The sounds, smells, textures, or any songs or movies that were playing in those moments. I used to think my experience was vastly different from hers and in a lot of ways it is incomparable. However, there are a lot of stark similarities. I also vividly remember everything. The smells, sounds, shadows and clothing. I remember the texture of the fabric of the sofa and her blanket. Breanne had a blanket that she kept with her and slept with every night. She called it the "Kiki blanket." It was a memento from her childhood that she had her entire life. She would wrap the blanket around her left hand and sink the tip of her thumb in her mouth. I would spend the next five years with her and that blanket.

Back to the movie. Breanne had grown concerned for my safety. I was an inner-city kid during a time in Buffalo where the murder rate was at an all-time high and I happened to go to one of the city's most notoriously violent schools. As I sat there on the couch, her head on a pillow, the pillow on my lap, a teenage boy's excitement under the pillow and me playing with her hair. The scene in the movie reached the part where the character Sam was shot and killed. She looked up at me and said, "I don't know what I would do if anything ever happened to you." We locked eyes for a moment and then I quickly nervously turned away. My heart was racing, knowing and feeling the desire for her. She laid her head back down and said to me, "You're such a fucking tease." That was the green light. At that moment, all doubts had been cast aside. I lifted her chin, our eyes locked again, and we kissed. That night we would not sleep together. That would happen about a week later. However, that night she did tell me that she wanted me since the night we had pizza, and she had been waiting for the chance.

Now, I want to clearly point out the lesson here. It is something I had not yet acknowledged until I wrote this book. That lesson is that I was the prey. Although my physical appearance would suggest otherwise, I was never in control. I never led the dance and never dictated the events that took place. I was the mouse, and she was the cunning cat toying with its catch. She was ferocious.

Step One Takeaways:

1) You did not do this to yourself. How could you? You were just a child.

2) Adults fail children, not the other way around.

3) Your abuser did not love you; love is on the opposite side of abuse.

Actions Toward Healing:

1) Participate in daily positive self-affirmation.

2) Find a trusted source to talk to.

3) Acknowledge what happened, don't bury the hurt.

Learn To Be Honest Again

"You ain't gotta lie to kick it."
— Kendrick Lamar

One of the many things victims learn to do very early on is to cover for and protect their abusers. There are many reasons for this. One is fear of retaliation. An example of this could be a victim reporting the abuse and having to suffer the wrath of the abuser later whether it be physically or emotionally. Another reason victims cover for their abusers is shame. This could be feeling undignified from being taken advantage of or falling yet again for the con. A victim could also cover for their abusers due to sheer embarrassment. Consider being young and knowing the stigma attached to being with somebody who wasn't really a good match with you physically. Young men can be ruthless if they think you are dealing with somebody who is not a banger in the looks department. Breanne wasn't unattractive by any means, but she wasn't a young teenage girl. Especially a teenage girl at Grover which housed a diverse student body of several different cultures. A victim could also protect their abuser due to a misguided sense of love or loyalty. When a victim is manipulated, they are essentially trained to look out for the abuser's well-being. It's like Stockholm syndrome, when a victim identifies with his or her abusers and develops positive and protective feelings toward them. Victims bond with their abusers to help cope with the trauma. Admittedly, I was not feeling like I was held hostage at the time. Those feelings came much later. Sometimes all those reasons take place simultaneously, but no matter the reason, we do it.

I can remember as a child, lying to Child Protective Services about the bruises and welts on my body to protect my father. I would make up stories and suggest that I'd fallen or that it was nothing. I can remember sitting in class fabricating stories about my happy home life for my friends so they wouldn't know what was really going on. I did that to protect the image of our family. I don't want this story to come off like an Eminem song where he relentlessly vents and goes in on his mother. I had a lot of empathy for mine.

My Mother's Lies

She was eighteen years old when she married my father. Eighteen and barely more than a child herself. From the start of that relationship, she was beaten daily, sexually assaulted, and controlled. For all intents and purposes, she was a victim, too. Her own backstory is quite tragic in its own right. In some ways she deserves a little grace, but that doesn't erase the damage she did. Me being empathetic also does not negate the fact that for me and my siblings she was a central figure in so much of the trauma we lived through. Much of that trauma spawned directly from deceit. My mother often asked me to lie for her. It really wasn't until I was damn near thirty years old that I finally began to understand the real reasons behind many of those lies.

One scenario in particular stands out. One day she asked me to pretend that I was attending school during my freshman year of high school for the purpose of deceiving my father. She told me to act like I was attending every day and to tell him that school was going fine even though I wasn't really there. It's crazy because I didn't even have school clothes. She told me she just needed me to pretend for a couple of weeks until she could come up with money to buy me something to wear. So, of course, I did it. I went along with the charade and lied to him. The issue was that my father wasn't an idiot. After a few days, he knew something wasn't right and discovered the truth. That was when he beat both me and her for the lies. At the time I thought he was just angry that I hadn't been going to school. That was bad enough, but years later I found out that was only half of it. The real reason for the lie? My mother spent up all the money he had given her that was meant for my school clothes. She squandered that money on something else entirely. That was our dynamic. The lies we were asked to tell were never really to protect us. Most of the time, *we* were the casualties of *her* deceitful actions.

My mother also had a way of bragging about the crimes she would commit. One day when I was in my twenties, we were sitting in my living room with some friends. My mother began to brag to one of my friends about how she'd spent that money for those school clothes. She laughed and said she used it on her "other man" during a coke and sex binge. That was it. That was where the money for my school clothes had gone and of course I suffered the consequences. I had essentially paid for that party both literally and figuratively. Not just with missing school. I'm talking about the embarrassment of having no clothes, no clean socks or underwear to wear in those first few weeks of the school year. I paid for it with my flesh. The wounds from that beating lasted a long time. On the other hand, my mother never even blinked. What's crazy is that years later at my father's funeral my mother who loved to try to cover her tracks and sell her side of a story even if unsolicited, randomly walked up to my new bride and casually said, "They didn't have it that bad growing up." She followed that up with the same conversation with my mother-in-law in the kitchen. Most of my new family members in the kitchen were Spanish speaking and barely spoke English. Yet, there my mother was, still selling wolf tickets. Wow. Minimizing at its finest. Thanks, Mom!

Now, on November 10th, 1995, in her candlelit living room with Sarah McLachlan's song *Ice Cream* playing softly in the background, I had sex with Breanne for the first time. Afterwards, we sat there in silence. Then she began to cry. "I can't believe what I just did," she said through tears. "I've violated everything I believe in. If anyone ever found out, I'd be in so much trouble." With that being said, I knew I had to lie to protect her. To protect us. To do what I had been trained to do for as long as I could remember. It wasn't really a big ask because I loved her. I didn't want to cost her anything. I wanted to keep her safe. To keep her happy. To preserve what little peace we found in what we would later come to call "The Twilight Zone." Our escape from the reality that I was a sixteen-year-old boy, and she was a twenty-five-year-old teacher at my school. But here is the stone-cold truth:

There was no love in that room.

She did not deserve to be protected, *I* did. The only thing my protection did was help her escape from time in a jail cell, or minimally, the unemployment line. There would be many more lies to come. One of the hardest parts of that period was lying to my friends. A few days later, deep in the middle of this secret affair, I started hearing rumors about a new kid at school. Handsome. Charismatic. Dressed differently from most. His name was Carl. I still remember the first time I saw him walking through the third-floor halls of Grover. Baggy button-down shirt, loose tie, fresh fade, books in hand. I walked up and said, "What's up?" It felt in my mind that it was like when Batman meets Superman for the first time. Two kids with their own backstories meeting at just the right moment. You could almost hear the gears of the universe lock into place when we shook hands. After that, the world felt...a little more right. We started hanging out in gym class and during lunch. Then Carl told me he'd started hanging out with some other guys he met. Out of all the kids at school he could have linked up with as the new kid, he ended up talking about my close friends, Russ and Jay. I knew then it was fate. Some things are just meant to be. Carl would go on to become the most loyal person I had ever known. To this day I'm grateful for everything he did for me back then and for everything he continues to do for me now.

Lies, Lies, and More Lies

Imagine this: You're sixteen, a male in a hyper-masculine environment. Girls like you. You're turning them down. You're absent from group events. You randomly disappear without explanation. No one understands your weird stories or your sudden indifference to all the attention you're getting. Naturally, the rumor mill starts turning. The one that stuck? That I was gay! Now, in the 90s, this was not accepted in the way it is now. That was a big deal back then. I told Breanne about the rumor. She said we could find a "mutually beneficial" solution. Her idea was that I should casually date someone. You know, not get into anything too serious. If I was to be seen with girls who were my actual age and act like a normal student, we would throw off suspicion and be able to still have our time in our Twilight Zone. So, I gave it a shot.

There was a girl that I really did like too. Her name was Ani and I would see her on the bus daily. She was beautiful, kind, sweet, and innocent. Ani and I had a study hall and physics class together and I finally worked up the nerve to speak to her. The strange thing is she already liked me as well. She joked that she had been asking her friend if she should approach me and we hit it off right away. We would spend hours at night on the phone, talking in study hall, and eating lunch together. I hated having to lie to her, but I was intensely drawn to the Twilight Zone. I would spend my nights there in that attic apartment living my other life. Ani was deeply religious and was set on not having any sexual contact of any kind until she was married. She stuck to that, and I respected it. The most we ever did was hold hands once at her mother's house and I remember thinking it was the sweetest thing ever. She was Breanne's polar opposite. Ani was morally sound, innocent, and kindhearted. There was not a malicious bone in her body. She had an angelic quality that would just draw everyone in. The sad thing is that I think she actually loved me. She used to write me letters and beautiful sonnets from her heart and in a normal world, she and I would have been a real couple. In her mind, we were a real couple. However, the cruel reality was she was merely a shield, and I hated that because I had real feelings for her. I hated lying to her by pretending that I was a normal teenager living a normal teenage life with a normal teenage girlfriend.

Ten years her senior, Breanne was insanely jealous of Ani. She could sense that I was not pretending when it came to her. She could see that Ani was someone I wanted to be with. Additionally, Breanne was jealous because Ani was genuinely a good person without an agenda that consisted of mind games and deception. One afternoon while I slept in her bed, Breanne had found a letter from Ani in my coat pocket and read it. I was startled awake by her crying. She told me to immediately cut ties with her, or it was over between us. So, that's what I did. I ended the relationship with Ani the only way I knew how...I lied. To this day I had wished I could have just told her the truth. I remember running into Ani a couple of years later and she wanted nothing to do with me. I had hurt her badly and I deserved that ire. This was always the solution to our problems. This was always the fallback response... to lie. To tell the lie, act out the part of the lie and ultimately, live the lie. I was indeed a liar. I held this position even in the face of my family, my friends, and my classmates. I lied to her family, coworkers and friends. Every single day, every single word, every single action was based on a freaking lie.

The question then becomes, how do you overcome something of that magnitude? For me, I had to learn not to fear the consequences of the truth. The lies I had been groomed to tell were not mine, but we carry those habits because we were taught to fear the truth. Believing that somehow the truth would harm us more than any lie ever could. That's the trick. In reality the lies cost me...and believe me, they were expensive! All the dishonesty not only cost me relationships, it also cost me self-respect, integrity, a moral compass, a sense of direction, the capacity to respect others, courage, and much more. All the lies for my mother. The lies for Breanne. Those lies were more dangerous and damaging than any truth I could have told. Again, I could never grasp this conceptually, being so young.

Tessa's Necklaces

That constant need to protect, lie, and cover things up opened the floodgates for many other acts of deception in my life. It became a cycle that turned into its own prison as I would tell stories to hurt and deceive many others. I used girls as human shields for the sake of protecting my abuser. Girls like Tessa. I met the very confident and very beautiful Tessa at a school event that was being held at Buffalo State University. I was a senior then and nearly two years into my affair with Breanne.

Now, I wasn't exactly known for smooth approaches and pick-up lines. In fact, I was completely awkward when it came to talking to girls. Well, girls my own age anyway. I was out of practice because I didn't really need to do it. I was already tied up. But for some reason with Tessa the words just flowed as smooth as the Nile River. As I was leaving the event, Tessa asked if I needed a ride home. She and a friend had a car, and I hopped right in. Being young with your own ride in that community was a huge deal back then. Instead of going straight home we ended up at Pizza Hut spending the entire night laughing, talking, getting to know each other. They dropped me off at home and the very next morning, Tessa called me.

Tessa wasn't a student at Grover. She went to a private, all-girls academy. She had her own car and her own money. She was the teenage version of a grown woman. She even smoked cigarettes. She gave off this tough, bad girl image but underneath all that she was really nice and quite sensitive. She was a good person that had a complicated home situation of her own. At the time, I was told this was going to be the perfect cover. Tessa was known at my school because of who her parents were, and we genuinely enjoyed each other's company, but once again, the ultimatum came.

The green-eyed monster in the form of Breanne began unleashing ferociously. It got to the point where she actually accosted Carl in the hallway at school one day. As he explained it to me, she was beet red, steaming with anger with a look in her eyes that he couldn't identify with at that age. That was grown woman jealousy he was attacked with. He was so caught off guard he said he thought he was in trouble for something. She said to him sternly, "Get in here," pointing to one of the rooms off the hallway. He nervously walked in and she followed right behind him and shut the door. She got right into his personal space and aggressively asked him, "What is that girl Tessa doing with *my* boy?" Can you believe that? *My* boy. The word, my, obviously meaning possession/ownership. The word, boy, obviously historically racist. Carl and I were boys. She referred to me as her *boy*. Racist White people described (and still describe) Black men as boys to suggest that they aren't full-fledged people and are essentially inferior. And for any of you who may be reading this and feeling that it may not have been racist in nature, I will offer you the alternative. If the word boy in this context wasn't wrapped in bigotry, it was laced with perversion, acknowledging that I was nothing more than an underage sex object. Take your pick. I argue that it was both. Perhaps, racist implicitly and sexually deviant explicitly.

After being posed with that question, Carl just froze and ended up telling Breanne that he hadn't met Tessa and didn't know anything about it. He tried to downplay it, but she knew better. The funny thing is that I remember Carl not being fully convinced that I was in a full-blown sexual relationship with Breanne. After that encounter, he was thoroughly relieved of any doubt. He told me himself, "Ain't no chick acting crazy like that if she's not getting

53

any...." So once again I had to cut ties with Tessa and dispose of another healthier, more appropriate relationship. But first there was something Breanne wanted. She needed money. She wanted a new car, and after a failed attempt at insurance fraud (more on that later), she asked if I knew any way to come up with cash. I told her about some of my old connections in the arms business and she told me to reach out and see what could be done. To pull off the deal, I needed front money to acquire the guns. Breanne demanded that I get the money from Tessa.

So, in typical fashion, I did just that.

Tessa didn't have cash, but she gave me some jewelry to pawn under the promise that I'd pay her back. Breanne took the girl's jewelry and pawned it. I met up with my connection whose father owned a gun store and gave him the money. He later met me at my house that evening and delivered about thirteen guns. I would then begin to sell them to the predetermined list of buyers and make a decent amount of money. I remember going to Russ and Jay's house with a stack of money. They asked where I got so much money and as usual, I lied. The problem was that after the deal was done, I was never given the money to pay Tessa back. So unfortunately, I had to lie once again. I still remember Tessa, frustrated, reaching out to me, asking for her necklaces back. There I was stuck in the cycle, under orders, in survival mode. I had to pretend to be callous and ignored her. I fell back to my default setting which was to tell more lies. Tessa didn't deserve that. I lied every day to my friends and anyone who cared about me. I had to pretend to be doing things I wasn't doing and pretend to be in places I really wasn't.

Adults Fail to Help

There eventually came a point when the lying stopped. Not because we suddenly became honest, but because everyone around us had quietly accepted the obviousness of our situation. All the adults around the situation knew, one hundred percent. That's what still stings. Our names became synonymous with one another. We basically began to get invited to places as a couple. People treated us as a couple. I never understood how no one stepped in or at least questioned things. At that point we weren't even close to getting caught, we *were* caught. People saw. People knew. People talked. Yet, people failed to help.

As I said, Weldon would play a role in this tale as would my mother. Weldon was a good man and sadly, he would pass away a few years back from asthma. I can still hear his breathing machine humming in the bedroom as he tries to regain his breath. Weldon also struggled with an addiction to crack cocaine, one that would see him frequently relapse. My mother resented him for that. He never had a steady job despite being an amazing mechanic and craftsman. Weldon could build or fix just about anything. However, due to his addiction and inconsistent income they fought about money frequently. Things would disappear and we would see him wide eyed and sweating, wiping his brow when he was high. He had his issues, but his intentions for us and my mother were good. He tried to be a good stepfather and the thing I learned most from him was not to judge. Weldon was another person that was proud of me and saw things in me that I couldn't see back then.

Breanne and I were together during the early days of caller I.D. and no cell phones. They were not accessible to everyone yet. That meant that Breanne would have to call me on the landline house phone. She would also pick me up from my house. In those days, Weldon always had the phone so whenever Breanne would call, she would tell him that her name was Stacy. Weldon was never one to pass the phone without a conversation and over time he grew fond of "Stacy," often talking about her and inviting her over. So, one day after the movie *Titanic* was released on video, "Stacy" came to my house. Clearly, a very grown woman arrived at the door and Weldon and my mother greeted her and exchanged small talk briefly before we went into my room. This was Netflix and chill before streaming was a thing. We "watched" *Titanic* for several hours before she departed in the evening. Weldon and mother knew she was an older woman. They also knew she worked at the school but still stood by and allowed my mother's seventeen-year-old child to enter that room with that grown woman. There were no safety nets for me, and I was once again failed by my protectors. Weldon would later figure out that "Stacy" was Breanne and not even bat an eyelash about it.

I'm not even going to pretend that we were convincing anybody that we had a regular teacher-student relationship. There was no subtlety to how we were moving. I remember Russ flat out asking me once, "Are you banging that teacher?" I denied it, of course. I knew I was lying. I had no choice. I was in too deep to stop. Here are some questions that still haunt me. Who was I lying for? Why did I hurt so many people who cared about me? Back then, I didn't think I had a choice. When your life is so intertwined with your abuser's life, they control not just your emotions but your access, your identity, and your hope for the future. You don't feel like you have any choice at all. With Breanne, I had a warm bed. I had attention. I had popularity. I had sex. I had access. I was surrounded by the city's elite. I was mingling with judges, lawyers, and political figures. I became friends with newscasters and reporters. It was intoxicating. The allure of power and success through association. It was the promise of a fast track to the life I thought I wanted. One very different from what I was born into, and she knew I was mesmerized by it all. Breanne knew my struggles. She knew my desperation. I saw her as a way out. I started to believe that I was better than everyone else because I was "different," as she told me so often. That's the illusion. See, for abusive men, which I later became, we are told, or we tell ourselves or those we abuse that we are nothing without them or they are nothing without us. I was made to feel that I would never be anything without her. If I lost her, I would be cast back to the ghetto. That I would be nothing more than another west side piece of trash.

Here is the hardest truth of all. I still struggle with honesty today. Even when I'm confronted by my wife about the smallest thing, my instinct is still to lie. It's automatic. Fortunately, I was blessed with a woman of principle in my life. A woman with conviction. A woman who holds me to the standard of truth and I love her for that. I've come to understand that the truth is okay. I now understand that it is the only way forward. The philosopher John Locke had a term, *Tabula Rasa*, that translates from Latin to mean "blank slate. This basically means that the mind is essentially a blank slate at birth and gets filled with experiences. I wasn't born a liar. I was made into one, and if you've been through something like I was, you were probably made into one as well. Here is what you need to hear: You don't need to be in survival mode anymore. There's nothing to fear. You are safe. You are loved. You can be honest. You can live your life without your abuser. You are stronger than they will ever be.

You are Doscriosta.

Step Two Takeaways:

1) Lying is not protection.

2) Lying only prolongs an issue.

3) Don't be afraid of the exposure truth can bring. The abuser taught you to lie to protect and hide them. You don't need to hide.

Actions Toward Healing:

1) Tell the truth. Don't fixate on the worst-case scenario.

2) You can only be ashamed of the truth if you know you're wrong. If you can't openly discuss it, don't do it.

3) Share your experience with people who may need it.

Find Your Identity

"I've missed more than 9,000 shots in my career. I've lost almost 300 games. 26 times, I've been trusted to take the game winning shot and missed. I've failed over and over and over again in my life. And that is why I succeed."
– Michael Jordan

When the Temple of Apollo at Delphi was discovered, the Oracle's temple was found to bear several inscriptions. One of them read, *"Gnothi Seauton,"* or in Latin, *"Temet Nosce,"* meaning, "Know Thyself." Another read, *"Meden Agan,"* meaning "Nothing in Excess." These were not casual sayings. They were imperative lessons for any hero about to embark on a quest. To face life's challenges, you needed to know who you were. To understand your limits. To master your strengths. Most importantly, it was necessary to avoid excess. Not just external excess, but the internal kind as well. Things like too much worry, fear, pride, timidity, and so on.

For those of us who were abused, we lose that sense of self. Our abusers shaped us and molded us into who *they* wanted us to be. I was a child. I had no idea who I really was or what I wanted from life yet. I thought what she wanted for me was what was best for me. I trusted her with everything I had but I couldn't have been more wrong. The person she actually wanted me to be was her father, and in a sick, Freudian way that was always her goal.

Alcohol

I remember my very first taste of alcohol. I was twelve years old. My father had a mistress named Gwen. As part of our crazy dynamic, not only did Gwen live with us but her kids did as well. A bunch of fake stepsiblings running around the house with us. My father and Gwen's relationship was no secret in my home and my mother had no choice but to comply. One night, Gwen approached me with a glass of liquid. It was pink and she said, "Here try this." I reluctantly grabbed the glass and drank it. I could feel the burning liquid down my throat as I swallowed the concoction of gin and pink lemonade. Later on, after being confronted by my big sister Chontra about why she handed a twelve year old an alcoholic drink, she simply replied, "He is tall." That is how it typically went for me. The abuses were always justified because of my height or some invisible aura of maturity I possessed. I was not aware that drinking came with a height sign like at the entrance for a roller coaster ride. You have to be this tall to drink this drink. Again, one of many justifications used to provide me with alcohol when I was well under the age.

Breanne loved to drink just as much as the rest of her cohorts. There would be many, many drunken nights. I don't think I ever really even liked alcohol and eight years into my sobriety as I write this, I often ask myself how did I ever make a single good decision being a teenager drinking so much? I think about how it started. We would sit in her apartment and first it began with a glass of wine when we had dinner then a beer or two as we watched movies. Eventually, we would begin going to gatherings where the adults at the party would ask me to "keep it between us" that they were serving me beer and drinks at the cookout. These were prominent members of the Buffalo community, and they operated with impunity. Who was I going to tell? They were the police officers, attorneys, and social workers, all of whom were supposed to be mandated reporters.

I would spend many nights in the bar *The Keg Kastle* located in Buffalo's famous Chippewa District. This was a place that her friend owned and her family frequented. A controlled environment that operated as an accessory to numerous misdeeds. We would go to other places too, where the people I was with would flash their badges to allow me access to strip clubs and cigar bars. I wanted to emulate these men. Their power and money were what I was being groomed to covet and for a moment, I believed that I was one of them, but was I, really?

Daddy Issues

Breanne would often ridicule and diminish my true self. She made me feel that my authentic self was not good enough. You see, I loved sports, hip-hop music, and in fact, I enjoyed being a little "ghetto." There is rich culture and tradition in "ghetto" communities, and a lot to be proud of. Amazing people have come from ghettos and I used to love the time I got to spend with my real friends, the Bomb S.Q.U.A.D. Halfway through my junior year, I was asked to come to Russ and Jay's house. They had been rapping together and recording mixtapes with Carl and Damon. Damon was already tight with Carl from their former high school. He was a cool, attractive, well-dressed guy with incredible rhyming and drawing skills and he fit right in. I was asked to join "The Squad" and contribute some verses to the latest tape, and I was beyond ecstatic! I had no real experience rapping aside from what Jacob had taught me, but I figured I would give it a shot, and I loved every second of it. We would spend hours listening to instrumentals, writing lyrics, practicing, and recording songs. Then we would head to the yard and play basketball until we could barely walk anymore. Some of the most legendary basketball games I had ever played were in that yard. It was our safe haven, and I am eternally grateful to

Russ and Jay's parents, the late Mr. and Mrs. Maxwell for providing that for us.

There is an honesty to growing up where I did. A truth that I enjoyed and clarity that I bask in. Breanne, however, did not feel that way and would often make remarks about rapping being "ghetto" and how it was a dead end. She never listened to a single song, nor did she care for it. Very hard pivot from sitting in her apartment with me acting like *Bone Thugs-N-Harmony* was the best thing she ever heard. She was a big fan of sports, though, but not because of me. I remember her relative joked once, "I see you finally got to date the high school quarterback!" as if I were making up for something she missed out on at an earlier point in her life. She only enjoyed sports because her father was an athlete. She enjoyed my success on the court or field because in some ways, she could take credit for it. If I celebrated a successful play too much, she would disapprove. She wanted me to be the reincarnation of her father, James, and everything I did had to meet that standard of what he would do.

It started small at first, like telling me to tuck my shirt in or get them a size smaller. Then it would graduate to her buying me clothes to wear to places so that I would "fit in better." Then she would constantly correct my speech because James was a stickler for proper English. She would correct the grammar on cards that I had given her or letters that I would write to her. To be fair, she was a teacher after all.

There was one moment that stood out above the rest. It was the day before Christmas Eve in 1995. We were sitting in her living room, and she was wrapping presents for her friends and family, and she opened the bottle of cologne that she had gotten for her father. "I love this scent." she said. "It is my absolute favorite." She sprayed some of the cologne on my neck and inhaled deeply. It seemed to turn her on in a way that was different than what I was used to. She began kissing my neck and the rest I am sure you can figure out from there. I should have been disturbed by that moment, but I was young and just happy with the end result.

Looking back now, it's clear that I was never really meant to be myself. I was being turned into someone else. Nothing more than a stand-in or off-brand replacement. She wanted me to be her father. The man she couldn't reach, couldn't fix, and couldn't have. The more I became a version of James in how I dressed, spoke, and moved through the world, the less I knew who *I* really was. That's one of the cruelest things about grooming and abuse. It essentially robs you of yourself. It convinces you that what you want, what you like, or even what you feel doesn't matter. The only thing that matters is who *they* want you to be, and if you're young enough, lost enough, hurting enough, you start to believe it, too. You take on that mask.

For me, the mask got heavier and heavier as the days rolled by. When I was out with Breanne, I had to be her man. The polished, controlled, proper version she could parade in front of friends, family, coworkers. When I was with my friends at Russ and Jay's house or on the basketball court, I could feel the cracks in that mask. In those spaces, I could almost remember who I really was. Almost isn't enough though. The mask always had to be put back on. After a while, you begin to forget which version of you is real.

Prey

The alcohol-centered activities continued to flow. The nights got longer, and we began to have more and more conflict. You see, the abuser needs to weaken you. There are a variety of predators out there in the wild. There is the king cobra with its instant death bite, or the mighty lion in the savannah. My predator was more like the Komodo dragon. They hunt by biting their prey and tracking them slowly. They watch them weaken from a wound that will never close and proceed to rot from the inside until they are too exhausted to fight. Then they are consumed. I was consumed. I was positioned to rot from the inside until it began to seep outward into all my actions, words, and thoughts. That rot devoured me from the inside and reshaped me into the abuser in the situation.

Self-loathing can manifest itself in many ways. I was an insecure, poor, Black kid surrounded by wealthy White men and women in places that I did not belong. Due to my age, I lacked the ability to articulate that and so I would resort to childish means like name calling. I often verbally abused Breanne during disputes, and it would only perpetuate the cycle of self-hate. What was wrong with me? Why did I act that way? I couldn't control myself sometimes. The part of me that despised her could not remain at the surface long enough to express why. I can admit why now, though, because deep down I knew what was happening. My soul tried to resist by utilizing all the weaponry it had been equipped with at that age, but my need for her to love me and to accept me kept drawing me back in. That is why I would continue to pretend. I pretended to be one of them when I was around them and pretended to be a normal teenager when I was around my friends.

The biggest revelation came for me one day while I was at Breanne's house during my senior year. I slept over and the doorbell rang. There was no escape from the attic apartment. It was a one-way-in-one-way-out setup, so I hid under the bed. It was her younger sister, Meg. She had been in a fight with a friend the night before and during the fight he punched her right in her eye. She was upset because her relative, who was a prominent government official at the time, had shown her badge to the police who arrived on the scene and permitted the friend (another member of Buffalo's elite) to leave without any repercussions. Meg sat on the bed weeping as I lay there motionless. She told the story and then asked if she could take a nap. Breanne obliged and Meg proceeded to fall asleep on the bed with me underneath it. I laid under there silently for four hours while she slept her pain away.

Wiping the Slate with a White Woman's Tears

Fast forward to about three years later as I am being escorted out of the holding cell at the Erie County Courthouse, accused of being a stalker, and watching that very same prominent government official prance through the courtroom to address the prosecutor in my case. To see the same sister who took that punch in the eye sitting with three other women—who had all taken advantage of me at one point or another—shielding a pedophile, truly showed me the privilege, audacity, and outright hypocrisy of these people. I was awestruck at how they banded together to send me to slaughter. I knew then that they were not punishing me for my crimes. They were punishing me for theirs. I received a very important reminder that day. I was not one of them, and the only difference between me and the judge was the color of my skin. When it was all said and done, she used the oldest, most powerful weapon in America against a Black man... a White woman's tears.

Prior to my arrest, I was lost. Breanne was all that I had and all that I had known. We were at a crossroads, and I craved to be accepted. See, we had an agreement that once

I graduated from high school, we would effectively end the relationship. For me deciding to end it may have been to branch off and meet someone more suitable. For her, it may have been to find new prey. That way I would be able to go off to college and live a normal college life. However, that would change days prior to me going away to school. Breanne called me sounding distraught. She stated that she needed to meet with me right away. She picked me up and we drove to the Burger King parking lot on Elmwood Avenue. She was sobbing and crying while telling me that she did not want it to end, that she loved me. I told her that it was not possible. I could not and did not want to continue to be her secret. We finally agreed to just be friends, and I left and went on to attend Daemen University in Amherst, NY, right outside of Buffalo.

My first weekend at the university, I was hanging out in the dorm and with a really cool group of people my own age I'd just met and enjoying a normal eighteen-year-old's college experience. When I looked to my left, I saw Breanne standing in the hallway of the dorm. She had been calling my room repeatedly and when I did not answer she arrived in person, upset because I did not accompany her to a wine tasting party at her friend's place. Keep in mind that I was the one who would be labeled as the stalker. The hypocrisy.

I remember another incident where I fell asleep while on the phone with her and was startled awake when I saw a foot coming through my window. It was her breaking into my room because she was "worried" about me. There would be more instances like this during my time in college with me feeling like I would never be able to escape. One day I called her, she did not answer and in my profanity-laced tirade I left on her voicemail, I told her to stay away from me or I would hurt her. I had totally lost myself from that whole ordeal that was disguised as a relationship. I went to her house and rang the doorbell but she did not answer. Instead, she called one of her political connections who picked me up and took me home.

Called to Serve

After my failed college basketball career, I was lying on my mother's sofa defeated and lost when a commercial for the Marine Corps flickered across the 20-inch TV. My foot was in a soft cast from a recent ankle injury, but something in me stirred. I limped down to the recruiting station and signed up. Ironically, I flew out to Parris Island on Breanne's birthday in October. She was ecstatic about the idea of me joining the military. Again, her "boy" doing one of those things that she could brag about to her family and friends. It would act as yet another way for her to accept credit for my choices and efforts while subverting my accomplishments. We talked about the possibility of having a real future together and in true stereotypical romantic-war-hero fashion, she wrote letters to me when I was in Parris Island. I really needed those letters. I looked forward to them and used them as fuel to persevere.

I'll never forget that first night. As the bus pulled up to bootcamp and I placed my feet on those infamous yellow footprints. They were right near the intake barracks. These were the same yellow footprints shown in every recruiting video. The ones that would mark our position in formation. The same yellow footprints that all of those recruits that had come before me stood on and the many, many after. I looked up to see a meteor shower lighting up the sky. Green streaks hissed through the night like electric scars. It felt like a sign from the universe.

I endured boot camp on that busted ankle swollen to the size of a softball until a final inspection. A captain looked down, shook his head, and said I'd need medical clearance to complete the Crucible. The Crucible is the "final exam" for all recruits in basic training. It is a grueling seventy-two hours of sleep deprivation combined with miles and miles of walking. There, soldiers do marches, combat simulations and obstacle courses. I begged the medical staff to allow me to participate. I pleaded my case and the fact that I'd made it as far as I had, and there was no way I was about to give up.

Thankfully, they let me through.

During that final push, we would sweat, we would bleed, we would endure. I walked those miles, climbed those obstacles and sweat and bled. The ankle would throb and my back would ache. However, I was not weakened. I was hardened in a way that maybe was the first hidden lesson for me. My first time tapping into my indestructibility.

I stood at the Iwo Jima monument, a symbol from one of the fiercest battles in World War II. Every Marine knows the tale of that monument, the moment when the red, white, and blue would rise on a hill by battered, bruised, but never defeated men. A testament to the training, heart, and spirit of the Semper Fidelis. I stood there proud of myself; no one had done this but me. As "God Bless the USA" played over the speakers, tears falling, I thanked them in silence. I made it. I was a United States Marine.

I came home on leave hoping that, now, I'd be worthy of Breanne's love. That she would finally claim me openly. However, somehow, I still remained a secret. Just a secret in one of the most prestigious uniforms that a person can don. Even during my twenty-eight days of leave, we were sneaking around. Still having sex in my mother's house like two kids in hiding. Her friends still wanted their share, and I drunkenly obliged.

When I deployed first to Virginia Beach and then to Okinawa, Japan as an intelligence analyst, I left as a broken man-child. My time in the fleet was filled with reckless drinking, womanizing, and suppressed rage. They trained my body, but they didn't train my soul. I carried my wounds along with me overseas, drank them down, and buried them deep inside myself. I was known for the parties, the women, and the overall wildness. But beneath the chaos, I was still just a boy still chasing Breanne's approval, still trying to matter. After three years of heavy drinking, I was reassigned to recruiter duty to finish out my military career. The Marine Corps determined that my alcohol use posed a security risk, disqualifying me from continued service in the intelligence field. I never completed that assignment.

I returned home from my final duty station in San Diego, California to Buffalo a legal adult, but inside I was still just that boy. Angry. Hurt. Desperate to be accepted. And unfortunately, she had already moved on. That was the beginning of many downward spirals. The Marine Corps taught me how to endure pain, but it didn't teach me how to process it. So, when the uniform came off, the last mask of control went with it.

I was lost yet again.

Her Pet Project

I also struggled with suicidal ideations during that time. I was constantly intoxicated, angry, scared, and depressed. I remember not feeling like I was good enough, conflicted, and lost. My insecurities overwhelmed me, and I only found solace in her. I needed her to feel complete, or at least I thought I did. Her wanting me was validation that I was worth something. I decided to give her an ultimatum.

If we were to be anything, it would have to be a real couple. I meant an out and well-known couple. She flat out rejected that notion. She always introduced me as her protégé, never her boyfriend. People always knew we were together but it was never spoken aloud. It was devastating.

So yes, I needed an answer and in pursuit of that answer, I pushed and pushed past what was considered legal. I remember sitting at a café, being warned by one of her politician friends that if I persisted, there would be consequences. I told him that I just needed to know why I wasn't good enough. The saddest part of that conversion was that he had known about her crimes but was still willing to be not only complicit in their cover up but to excuse her behavior. He said to me, "Well, you were seventeen at the time you slept with her" as we sat in the little cafe on Elmwood as if that made it better. That somehow because I was at the age of consent in New York State at one point in the relationship, any sitting city court judge would find that to be acceptable. Despite me telling him, a court official, that I was the victim of crime, he would do nothing. She was protected and I was expendable. She was somehow the victim and that enraged me. First off, I was sixteen when we first had sex, not seventeen. Second, there was a power dynamic due to her role as a teacher in my high school. Even the probation officer who interviewed me for probation remarked in his findings that I was "remorseless." Yes, I was because the revelation came to me in that interview that I was indeed the victim in this situation. Yet, she was the one that was being protected.

This is what we fear and what we all know. This is why we stay silent and why we don't feel like we belong in this world. I was nothing more than a toy to them. Not just her, to all of them. A plaything. Like she told Carl when we were in high school, a "boy."

I had no identity outside of her and her circle. I was their pet project, plaything, or maybe just a justification that they weren't racist, you know, that whole "I can't be racist because I have a Black friend" thing that goes on. I was their shield from their own hate. Nothing more than a talking penis for many of the desperate housewives in the circle. Someone to showcase and something to mold. That sense of worthlessness did not escape me for a very long time. I would struggle with alcoholism, sex addiction, and marijuana addiction. I would never seek love, closeness, or companionship. I would only seek lust, superficial things, and immediate gratification. I was consumed by the shame of being labeled a stalker. The weight of being a convicted criminal and the pain of never being good enough for someone I loved was daunting. She didn't lose anything. She didn't lose a friend, a moment of sleep, and still, to this day, has her career as a teacher. Her indiscretions were hidden behind the veil of her false victimhood and her cohorts were more than willing to acquiesce to that facade. I wonder how many others there have been over the years.

I Am Doscriosta

Here is what they didn't know or probably weren't prepared for: I am Doscriosta. Indestructible. A walking force of nature. Yeah, I was down but never broken. I was not going to go gently into the night. The title of this chapter is "Finding Your Identity" and so that was my quest, to obtain the knowledge of self. Who was I? I was a child in a man's body. So, I explored like a child. You see, we forget that the only way to move forward is to know the position in which we were lost. I was sixteen years old, so I started over from that age. I explored all my interests, games, food, and travel. I found a niche for myself in an industry and slowly began to find my voice, to find my *self*. Ironically, I also discovered that I love to teach. However, I did not want to be a teacher. I was great at sales and collections. So, I taught and trained people in those areas. I found myself, my path, and my guiding principles through the ever-persistent strength that coursed through my veins. I was able to travel the world, obtain financial success, and most importantly, meet the love of my life. That same grit, passion, and work ethic is what drives me. Not for vengeance or retribution but for me, my child, and my wife.

I ended up seeing Breanne once some years ago in a restaurant while I was out with a friend. She walked into the restaurant we used to frequent together and the place where she had got me a job once. As she walked in, we made eye contact as she sat down with her companion and once she realized it was me, she began to stare. She looked at me and I could see her sad, teary-eyed gaze and it meant absolutely nothing to me. I promptly paid the check, left, and went on with my life. No more chasing her validation, no more seeking approval. I had my own. To become a man, I had to allow the child to grow. I had to let him play, feel, and live. Through him, I raised myself from the ashes into a man that today is beloved, respected, and admired. I am TaJuan Williams.

Step Three Takeaways:

1) Know yourself and be yourself no matter what.

2) Respect the tremendous value that the *real* you offers the world.

3) Do what makes you feel good about yourself.

Actions Toward Healing:

1) Engage in healthy activities of your choice.

2) Don't live for others. It's ok to have your own wants.

3) Find a compass, a guiding philosophy, or way to live. Find a purpose.

Find Your Peace

"You gotta find peace within yourself. If you can't,
then there's nothing nobody else can do."

– Tupac Shakur

Even with my grand gesture of walking out of that restaurant without incident after seeing Breanne, I did not walk out of that restaurant as a healed man. I wasn't even close to being fully restored at that time in my life. At that point I was still in a mess of addiction, depression, womanizing, and self-loathing. I hadn't even reached the worst of it yet, which was my arrest, and even that wouldn't be the last time I would wear handcuffs. My interview with that probation officer? Not the last time shame would pin me to a chair. There would be many more days like that. Cold lonely nights and piles of regrets to carry. What haunted me the most wasn't just what had been done to me. It was what I had done to myself. I was drowning in shame. I couldn't talk about it with anyone. I carried the crushing weight of failure everywhere I went including the thoughts that I wasn't good enough, that I was damaged, and ruined overcame every fiber of my being. Breanne and her circle had taught me that I didn't belong anywhere, and I had no identity of my own.

They isolated me from my family, my culture, and my friends. I wasn't "TJ" anymore, I was nothing more than a project. The little ghetto boy that she saved. Best believe that her friends wanted a piece of the action, too. At *the Keg Kastle*, I was a running joke. A toy passed around to be played with. The punchline to the inside jokes they told during their private group's stories. Softball games, beers, wings, it didn't matter. Every night ended the same for me, which was being in the bed of another one of her friends. A new volunteer. A new person's turn. It went on like this for over a year. They didn't know me. They didn't care. I was a novelty. A slave fantasy. A "boy." A marionette played with for amusement. I was desperate to feel and be seen as a real person but no matter how hard I tried, Breanne would never give me that.

Laying the Bricks of Reality

The hardest thing to shake wasn't the shame, it was the guilt. I believed that I ruined everything. If only I had been better, if I hadn't sworn so much, if I had dressed better, if I had been more patient then maybe I could have preserved the relationship. Maybe I wouldn't have lost everything.

I blamed myself for what happened. For all of it. That guilt made me restless, sad, and ashamed. Every day I walked through life carrying that regret like a storm cloud hovering over my head, afraid to speak my truth. Terrified someone would find out. Terrified they would say out loud that I was a crazy stalker. Will Smith once said, "When you go to build a wall, you don't just show up and build a wall. You have to lay one brick at a time and lay that brick as perfectly as possible." This is another thing the abuse can take from you, peace. Therefore, I had to build my wall of peace. Unbeknownst to me it would take me another twenty years to build. I didn't have the clarity to process it all at the time and in the midst of it, I could not discern the illusion from reality. My first mistake was calling it a relationship. My first brick to lay was the reality brick. I had to realize one very fundamental truth. That is that I was not in a relationship with my teacher. I was the victim of a child predator. What looked like affection was really a cage. I was not a person involved in a relationship; I was prey. Prey that was groomed by someone hiding behind a trusted title.

That foundational piece helps to start that process. It took a long time for me to understand this basic reality. I was not wrong; I was done wrong. I was not crazy; I was the victim of insanity. I was not weak, sad, or lost. I was left for dead and had to fight my way back out of the darkness to salvation. Doscriosta. The self-loathing had also taken quite a toll on my life. I would continue a self-destructive pattern that would lead me to hell again through homelessness and suicide attempts.

One day, before the first time I was arrested, I sat in a room entirely alone for two days straight. It was just me, a bottle of Jack Daniels, and a revolver. I remember being on the phone with Carl drunk out of my mind. I had placed a bullet in that gun and spun the chamber and snapped it into place. I then put it to my head, pulled the trigger, and heard the click of the empty chamber. I dropped the gun out of the window. It fell behind the dumpster in the back of the building and out of nowhere the police arrived at the house took me to the Comprehensive Psychiatric Emergency Program (CPEP), the infamous psychiatric ward at the Erie County Medical Center.

Carl had saved my life. Immediately after hearing how I sounded during that phone call, he contacted the police and told them where to find me. Based on his own experiences, he was able to assess the situation and recognize that it wasn't just another drunken night for me. He knew that something was different. Something was off. I am grateful he made that call. I was in a dark place, and had there been no intervention, it would have only been a matter of time before I went down to that dumpster to retrieve that gun and take my own life. My time in the hospital was my first shot at being sober. There I would meet Dr. Naz and gain some clarity before being released into custody of two City of Buffalo detectives who had a warrant for my arrest for stalking Breanne. You see, the day I had gone to her house, after her politician friend took me home, she went straight to the police station leaving me unaware that the final domino had already tipped. I did not realize it at the time, but that previous conversation in the café was an actual heads up that this was going to be the consequence. The rest you already know.

I know it may sound cliché, but it took me a long time to lay the next brick which is love of self. I had to learn to love me. The *real* me for all my gifts and for what I could offer the world. Once I realized that I was not crazy, I was able to understand that I was hurt. I was not broken, I was damaged. This meant that if I could stand, I could walk, and if I could walk, I could run. But to truly understand how I got here, I need to take you back a few steps. I had to reflect on the many moments when it was made clear to me that I was nothing more to Breanne than something to use. At the time, I couldn't fully grasp the gravity of it. I didn't yet understand why I was trying so hard to numb that pain, drown it with alcohol, chase it with sex, and run from it anyway I could. One of those moments sticks with me. You'll see why.

Breanne needed a new car. She had an old Jeep Wrangler and wanted to get rid of it. The problem was that selling it wouldn't bring in enough money and an insurance claim would pay much more. So, what was her plan? The usual. To call in her "boy" and his other Black friend, Carl. The plan was simple. She would leave the Jeep parked somewhere. We'd "steal" it, stash it somewhere, and set it on fire. She would then collect the insurance money and if anything was left, she would throw us a little cash. She was even gracious enough to allow us to joyride for a while and let her know when we were done before she called the police. Wasn't that nice of her? But there was one problem. Carl didn't know how to drive a stick shift! I couldn't help much either because I wasn't driving at all yet. It didn't matter, though, because in her mind we were "inner city kids" so, of course, we would know how to pull off a job like this. It should be second nature, right? She expected us to be experts in crime as if it was a genetic predisposition. Carl and I started doing the research. Mind you, this was before Google and the internet in general was readily available to everyone. We were trying to figure out how to pull off the scam, but it was taking too long, and Breanne got impatient. She was upset at the fact that we were not ready and willing and/or able to drop everything and commit insurance fraud for her for maybe a few dollars. Since we were taking our sweet time trying to figure out how to pull it off without getting ourselves into trouble, she opted to do it herself. She must have watched too many movies beforehand because she ended up taking a screwdriver and jamming it into the ignition. Obviously, it didn't work. It just left her with a wrecked ignition and an expensive repair bill. Looking back, it all could have gone wrong and she would have left us out to dry for grand theft auto and insurance fraud while her relative would have cleared her. Then Carl would have been dragged into the sick power dynamic that I was suffering in. I am so glad he couldn't drive that Jeep.

Twilight Zone of Hell

Like so many others, that moment drove the truth deeper into me. I was always good enough for sex. Good enough to do her dirty work. Good enough to be paraded around to boost her image and to show off what a "project" she had polished, but never good enough to be her actual significant other. Not then. Not ever. I would never be anything more than her "boy." The Twilight Zone sounds like a place of serenity and an escape from reality, but as Rod Serling intended, it was a place of hard truths and nightmares. In truth, I was never escaping when I was with Breanne in that Twilight Zone. I was trapping myself, locking myself into a prison of false hope and chasing an unachievable goal. That one day she would truly love me. That is the twisted goal for so many of us. We so badly want our abusers to love us back. We want them to feel for us. To value us. To choose us. We want it so passionately that we strip away pieces of ourselves. Like Shel Silverstein's *Giving Tree*, we offer our fruit, shade, bark, branches, until nothing is left but a stump. Stripped completely bare, hoping that somehow love will grow again from what little remains.

Finding Love for Myself

Despite all that was going on and as rare as they were, I still had moments of peace. When I was with the Bomb S.Q.U.A.D., I could breathe. When I was on the basketball court, I was free. I didn't need a Twilight Zone to escape to. I had the real thing, but she even wanted to take those things from me. Rapping was one of my first true tastes of peace and sometimes I still wonder what life might have looked like if I had been able to pour my heart fully into it. To really become great. The time I spent with my peers, kids my own age, living normal lives, is what kept me afloat. I had a family. A brotherhood. A group of young men who loved me unconditionally and who stood by me when it mattered most. Carl and Jay put money on my books when I was locked up. Russ opened his home and let me break bread with his family. They were the roots of my peace. The basketball court was another place of salvation because there I was good enough. Respected. Wanted. Celebrated. I could fly on the basketball court and the only show I had to put on was the one I chose for myself. So where did I find my love of self? It didn't come instantaneously. Like most things that matter, it was a slow, painful realization that self-love was the product of many moments, not just one. The first of those moments came through my daughter.

Tali was born on a beautiful sunny December day in Miami, Florida. At first, her love for me was difficult to comprehend and to be honest, almost unbearable. She was such a wonderful, loving child and I believed I did not deserve anything that beautiful. She began to break me down, piece by piece. One day, when Tali was five and right in the middle of what was the absolute nadir of my existence, she placed her tiny hand on my cheek and asked me, "Daddy, why do you hate yourself?" My self-loathing was that obvious. It was so visible that this innocent little child had no choice but to inquire about it. It didn't totally change me that day but something inside me began to wake up. The wheels started to turn. My Tali did that for me and I can't even articulate how important she has been to my survival. The wheels started to turn a little faster after I found myself walking along the highway, hoping to be struck by a car until a New York state trooper found me and took me to jail. Nonetheless, the wheels continued to pick up a little more speed. More momentum came as I sat in the rehab center at Conifer Park located in Glens Falls, New York. Each lesson, each dark moment, each narrow escape began to add up until finally, the real revelation took hold. I had finally found peace. The calm mind and soul allowed me to then focus on the path to success. To grow from the stump, with clarity, purpose and vigor.

I was worthy. Worthy of life. Worthy of love. Worthy of peace. And in surviving it all, I found the love of myself. Pressure makes diamonds or dust, and I was indeed a diamond. However, simply surviving wasn't enough. Now I had to learn how to really live. How to build something real out of all the broken pieces I had carried for so long. One brick at a time.

Step Four Takeaways:

1) You lived through the storm. The sunshine feels good.

2) Peace is more than silence. It's a lifestyle.

3) Don't judge others. Uplift and support the people around you.

Actions Toward Healing:

1) Relax. What is there to stress about after you have survived this? There is no situation that you are not prepared to deal with or can't overcome. Don't sweat the small stuff.

2) Cut them off so you can grow. Anyone who isn't about peace does not need to be around you.

3) Protect your space.

You Have Survived, Now Start Living

"You never know how strong you are until being strong is your only choice."
— **Bob Marley**

My Uncle Grady, my father's brother-in-law, for whom I have tremendous respect, once told me, "The hardest thing to do in life is to just die. You can't just lay down, quit, and say 'OK, I want to be dead,' so you might as well live." This was the same Uncle Grady that encouraged my love of basketball, chess, and politics. Grady was another flawed man who worked hard to become the best version of himself. There was no one more upset than he was after he found out I got arrested for the situation with Breanne. He tried to push my mother to pursue statutory rape charges against her, or at least do something, anything, but my mother chose to do her usual nothing. He couldn't have been more right. At the time,

I didn't understand what living even meant. I only knew how to survive. How to fight another day. How to numb pain, avoid consequences, and keep the mask on. That's survival. Living was something different; it would take me many years to learn that.

On my wedding day, standing as the man I had finally become, I would thank my uncle. His words were the spark that lit the fire for the long road ahead. Growing up, we were taught the bare minimum. No one showed me how to apply for a job, how to balance a checkbook, or even how to pay a single bill. Breanne, an adult, a teacher from a prominent family had done no better. In fact, she showed me even less. You see, an abuser doesn't want life for you. If you learn how to live you might learn to live without them and their narcissistic personalities can't handle that. Your dependency empowers them. Your perceived weakness acts as their fuel. Breanne would often remind me of my weaknesses and for years I thought she did it to help me or to motivate me to be better. I was terribly mistaken.

Some People Want You Small

Later in life, I would find myself in another relationship with the same pattern. A partner who wanted me to stay small. To only make enough to cover half the bills, to lower my expectations, to just be a stay-at-home dad. The more I tried to grow, the more resistance I felt. I see it clearly now. Both of those women wanted the same thing: the version of me that only knew how to survive. Remember this: A man who learns to live cannot be controlled.

With Breanne, there was always an undercurrent of racism. A quiet but constant weapon she used to control me and stunt my ability to live fully. I can recall one night after a game against Bennett High School. I had one of the most explosive slam dunks of my life. It was a vicious throwdown right in the face of one of their best defenders. The gym erupted. Teammates chest-bumping me, the crowd went crazy. It was an absolute frenzy! In that moment of raw joy, my teammate Marcus and I did a little victory dance we made up. Just kids celebrating their love of the game. Later that night, Breanne made sure to let me know how disappointed she was. "Real winners walk away and act like they've been there before," she said. "You looked like a loser, dancing around like that." What she really meant and what I didn't see clearly then was, "Don't be too Black." The same thing happened after a football game where I threw the longest touchdown pass of my career. I cleared about eighty-four yards on that throw! I remember watching the ball spiraling and soaring through the air, landing right in the hands of my teammate Jeff as he strode effortlessly into the end zone. Touchdown! After the play, I flashed the "number one" hand sign in a small moment of pride. That's all she seemed to remember from the whole game. Another lecture followed about humility, grace, and how I needed to "carry myself better." Game after game,

I became paralyzed by her disapproval, afraid to be too flashy, too joyful, too proud, too me. Afraid to draw her ire for being too Black. Afraid to disappoint her by not being her father, James.

Gatekeeping My Culture, Gatekeeping Myself

There were other instances as well. One of the most infamous nights in Bomb S.Q.U.A.D. history and a night that would lead to us recording one of our most coveted and legendary songs titled, *Stupid Bitches*. We had all gone to the movies with a group of girls known in our school as the 13 Clique. They were the 13 most popular girls in the school and boy, did they know it! We first tried to have pizza and were kicked out of the once famous spot, *Prima Pizza*, in downtown Buffalo due to the unruly behavior of the girls. Then we attempted to see a movie, but their foolishness got us booted from the movie theater as well. After that we attempted to go and play pool at the popular spot, *The Hippodrome*, and guess what? Correct, we were thrown out there, too. We returned to Russ's house angry and frustrated and found relief in a beat that we had been waiting to use and the lyrics had taken care of themselves. Living in the moment, carefree spittin' our truth, our experience, and to be honest, it was funny to us. I wanted Breanne to hear the song, and of course, she dismissed it as ghetto. A ghetto song about ghetto girls.

It wasn't just music or sports. If I wore the clothes I liked, they were criticized as "too baggy." If I used the language of my friends, I was instructed to "speak properly." Rap? "Ghetto." She did listen to rap music loud enough to be heard but never in a way that truly honored it. It was about being seen as cool and "down" with the culture, never about understanding it. She loved the image of the White girl with edgy taste with the "different" Black kid around. But it was never my truth. Never the story behind the music, behind me. In public, I was nobody. Or at best, merely her student. Privately, I was a body. Someone to use sexually and emotionally when she wanted and then pushed back into the shadows when it didn't serve her. What an awful human being.

To her friends, it was pseudo evidence she wasn't racist. "See you guys? I hang out with him." "He's cool." "He's not like the others." That was what I became. Not like the others, not like my friends at school and not like her friends at the bar. I was on an island when I wasn't with my brothers. I had no place, no identity other than her. So, to survive I played the role that gave me the best chance of survival which was to be the old White man she wanted in the young Black shell she desired. Even when we went out, it felt like she was parading me around as her polished project. The little ghetto boy she had saved, but was never allowed to be too proud, too free, too Black. That's what she wanted to erase and for a long time, I let her. I disconnected from my joy, from my friends, from the culture that gave me life. It would take me years to realize that reclaiming my voice, my pride, and my culture was not an act of rebellion. It was survival. It was healing. It was becoming whole again.

Numbing the Pain Through Addiction

The other means of survival we lean on is numbing feelings. It's like Novocain for the soul. In my case, it was alcohol. Later, marijuana. Whatever dulled the pain long enough to get me through the next moment, the next hour. The irony was thick. With Breanne, me being "too Black" was a sin but playing into Irish stereotypes was perfectly acceptable. What is more stereotypically Irish than drinking? She loved to drink. Everything, and I mean everything began and ended with alcohol. Good day? Let's drink. Celebration? Let's drink. Bad day? Drink. Dinner? Drink. Movie? Drink. As a child, because I was still a child, no matter how tall or mature they claimed I looked, I learned that alcohol was a tool. The alcoholic was the man slumped alone at the end of the bar but if you were at a gathering with friends, you were just unwinding. You were relaxing, taking the edge off, celebrating life. That was the lie and it was easy to believe, especially when the so-called responsible adults around you repeated it often enough. I watched not only them but Russ and Jay's parents, my parents, aunts and uncles, her parents and all of the teachers at school use alcohol as a means to an end. So naturally, it became my crutch. My coping mechanism and eventually, my cancer.

Numbing is not living. It's barely even surviving. It's dragging your battered spirit from one day to the next, never healing, never resting. The more I numbed, the less of me there was left to save. I would spend the next twenty-two years of my life as an alcoholic. Countless nights spent in bars and strip clubs, alone or surrounded by fake friends with a glass or bottle pressed to my lips, poisoning my body and soul. Eventually, I was a frail one hundred fifty-three pounds, sick all the time and lonely. I had burned every bridge and hurt and pushed away everyone who cared about me. As bad as I was with alcohol, I was worse with the marijuana. Before I arrived at Conifer Park, I had convinced myself that I wasn't an addict. I just needed to "cut back a bit." Addicts were junkies who did things like heroin, crack, and methamphetamines. Weed was just a plant. No one got addicted to plants, right? Like that famous scene from the movie *Half Baked* when Dave Chappelle's character stands up at a Narcotics Anonymous meeting and tells everyone that he's addicted to weed. The crowd boos him and shuts him down because he is not considered to be a real addict.

I believed that myth even though I was smoking an ounce a day and drinking a bottle of Jack Daniels daily, chased with beer after beer, living in perpetual inebriation or hangover. Even through all of that I still didn't consider myself an addict. A big part of that denial was because I had done well in life. I was a successful entrepreneur. I made money and had things most people only dreamed about. I had overcome that setback from my youth and built a life. Beneath all of that, though? I was still that wounded boy plagued by insecurities that had been carved into my DNA from the abuse. Anytime someone questioned me or challenged me I would fall back into the darkness. I got married and had a child, but that marriage was poisoned by my own untreated wounds, verbal abuse, strategic manipulation, and the toxic patterns I'd learned for survival. My ex-wife was another woman who never really loved me. The similarities to Breanne were staggering. She was proud of me in the same performative way. Her racism was subtle, and her family's racism was not.

I remember her hesitation in telling her father and her very racist stepmother that she was marrying a Black man. Her father literally asked, "Well, how Black is he?" She told him I was "mixed." His response? "Oh, he's an Oreo!" In that moment, I became an "acceptable" type of Black person in his eyes. I would go on to endure and rage against many more moments of that kind of bigotry from her family, but the most painful part was her refusal to acknowledge it. That silence was deafening. Still, I was a coward then. Rather than confronting the truth or leave, I stayed. In doing so, I made life unbearable for both of us. I can't absolve myself from her pain either. Every good moment we shared was inevitably offset by an abusive one.

Yet again I was "the prize." Nothing more than a walking, talking trophy. The Black man whose presence proved how progressive they were. Even the appearances of Breanne and my ex-wife were similar. We fought constantly. We were total opposites in every way and the relationship was filled with the constant reminder that in her and her family's eyes I would never be quite as smart or capable as the White men they admired. I had placed myself right back in the same condescending environment with the same type of person. That marriage collapsed and I ran headfirst into a wild, single life full of fast cars, fast women, and rivers of booze. That was until I no longer enjoyed it. Until life wasn't fun anymore. I was pretending again. Surviving. I had no concept of living. I was a husk of a man acting out what I thought a good-looking, successful single man should do and, of course, that house of cards collapsed soon, too. So, there I was, penniless, freshly released from jail and all alone in rehab at Conifer.

The only real difference between her and Breanne was that she, too, had come from a broken home, marked by abuse, addiction, and neglect. Before having our daughter, she suffered through several miscarriages. We both suffered through those miscarriages. For that, I genuinely admired her strength and perseverance. Other times, I resented her for it. Her instincts for self-preservation were powerful. They were almost too powerful, and I became an expendable part of that survival. In saving herself, she sometimes left me behind. Again, the truth is that I was too afraid to confront the reality of the situation. I remained complacent and ended up making life unbearable for both of us. We were like oil and water, but she did not deserve the abuse I inflicted upon her. I remember her once saying that she wished I had the decency to just punch her in the face because the verbal assaults hurt so much worse. Damn.

After four months of sobriety from my incarceration, my mind had begun to clear, and this time, my objective was simple. I wasn't just there to quit using. What gave me that clarity? Truthfully, it wasn't one moment, it was a thousand quiet ones. Nights I didn't want to wake up. Mornings I forced myself to. Friends I lost. My child I almost disconnected from. There wasn't a lightbulb. It was more like a slow, reluctant sunrise.

I began to reflect on my mistakes, my habits, my patterns. I looked in that chunk of polished metal on the bathroom wall in the cell block that they called a mirror and saw a battered and bruised man. However, I was still a man and despite everything, I was still here. Still breathing. And then came one question. And in my head, it sounded like the voice of Jigsaw from the movie:

"Live or die. You decide."

I chose to live. I started to believe my life still had weight. Still had worth. That even if they tried to bury me, they forgot I was a seed. I was a skinny, ragged mess. Step one was a haircut. My physical appearance had to start mattering again. A fresh cut for a fresh start. Even now, I go to the barber regularly to keep that rhythm alive. Then I started working on my body, believing that if I could take care of myself physically, maybe my mind would follow. One hundred push-ups became one thousand. Twenty-five pull-ups turned into two-hundred fifty.

As I grew stronger in body, my mind started to follow. My spirit began to rise. One day, I was sitting at a table in Erie County Correctional Facility, playing spades with four other inmates. We started talking about all kinds of things. Eventually, we got into history—one of my favorite subjects. I'm a huge history buff. Astronomy too. That conversation changed something. I saw that I had their full attention. Later, a few of them came by my bunk to talk more. Soon, we were holding daily meetings to talk about science, history, and ideas. I found that although these men had committed crimes, they were intelligent and insightful. Their minds weren't lost. They were just buried under pain like mine had been. Even though I'm not the most religious person, I took time to participate in prayer circles and Bible study. It helped me sharpen my understanding of where some of them were coming from. It grounded us in something deeper. We started tutoring sessions. Sharing what we knew. Listening. And that's when I realized something I had never seen before:

I was a leader.

As my mind cleared, the world looked different. I could laugh without weed or alcohol. I could sleep. I could eat. I felt less anxious. My thoughts became steady. Coherent. Calm. So when I finally found out the date of my release, I didn't just walk out.

I walked out with a plan.

I was there to learn how to finally be sober. To stop surviving and to finally start living. While in rehab, I was determined to work on both my mind and my body. Physically, I was strong. I had rebuilt my frame and became powerful again. Then I needed to become mentally powerful. I stood out in the rehab center not because I was the smartest man there but because I was taking it seriously. I approached it with a life and death type of seriousness. I loved group therapy. I was usually the first one in the room. Eventually, the staff allowed me to help run some of the group sessions. The therapists appreciated my candor and for the first time, I began to understand a simple but life-changing truth: I was not alone. Just like the men I had met in jail, I started to notice a pattern. You see, every man in that room was in pain, too. Different causes and different stories, but the wounds ran just as deep. They, like me, chose silent suffering and acts of aggression as a cry for help as a means of self-preservation. Some of them were the life of the party, others were the center of the pity. Like me, they had all sought salvation through their substance of choice. That's when another myth was shattered for me: I wasn't better because my substances were alcohol and weed. That didn't matter. Alcohol and weed found me just like crack and heroin found them. We were all using the same tool to survive. Numbing. And beneath it all, the common thread was the same fear of life. I learned to no longer fear the exposure or to run from the pain. For the first time in my life, I was willing to feel it, embrace it. I remember bringing the room to tears when I shared my real, whole, and complete story with the group. The tradition at Conifer Park was a testimonial, to write out and reveal things about yourself. It hurt like nothing else I had ever felt before and I truly learned that life can be painful, but pain is the weakness that leaves the body. That's why I have always loved the Saiyans from *Dragon Ball Z*. They get stronger through fierce battles, and they rise more powerfully after every hardship. I began to see that in myself. As much as life would beat on me, as much as the world might still try to tear me down, I realized that the one person who did not need to contribute to that pain…was me.

Nothing to My Name but My Name

I left the rehab without a dollar to my name, but I was not worried. I had no home to go to, and later, I would learn that my daughter would get on the school bus every day and cry about her homeless father. However, I was undaunted. I went to the welfare office to seek some sort of emergency assistance, but I was denied. It didn't matter. It was a minor setback. I had a phone, and I had me and my experience. I grabbed my garbage bag of clothes and walked to the bus station a block or two from the welfare building. I would call that bus station home for the next three weeks. I would spend my nights there sleeping with my bag of clothes. I had to move from terminal to terminal to not arouse suspicion and sleep in two-hour increments. In the mornings, I would stash my clothes in a locker there and wash myself in the bathroom of the Tim Horton's coffee shop down the street. I would occasionally eat out of the dumpster there. I got the Buffalo jobs newspaper and began calling around. I secured an interview one day and walked the twenty-two blocks to the location and secured the job. I would walk to and from that place for $13.00 per hour for the next three weeks until payday. I cashed that check with pride and I can still remember the first hot shower that I got to take in that crappy motel room I rented. I can still feel the water on my skin, hot, refreshing, and relieving. The bed, oh, the bed! The first one I slept in felt like I was laying directly on heaven's clouds. As gross as that room would be for me today, at that moment, the room was paradise. I would work there for another two months until phase two was ready. That was to find a better job and soon I did that too. What I did not expect was to find what I would find in the break room one day while refilling the Keurig.

She came into the break room and while I waited for the coffee to brew, we said an awkward, "Hello." Her name was Tiana, and I would later write this on our wedding website:

The butterfly effect is a theory that says a butterfly flapping its wings in one part of the world could set off a chain of events that could lead to a hurricane in another part. Who knows when the butterfly flapped its wings and set things in motion. What tiny breeze pushed us in the direction towards being together. I don't know what caused the Keurig in the breakroom to not have enough water in it. That lack of water kept me there long enough to meet a shy, beautiful woman reaching for more creamer for her coffee, exchanging an awkward hello. Or being seated in the cubicle next to her during training because none of the other computers worked and being offered a Snickers mini candy bar. It's the little things that lead to two people discussing burgers and hearing of a place nearby that sold amazing ones. Those small choices or missteps (or what we think are missteps) that lead to a clumsy man falling on the ice and knocking himself out which prompted a lunch buddy to get his phone number from a mutual friend and ask if he is ok. Those subtle glances and magnetic pull drawing two people together every day with every small choice that unbeknown to them would one day create a full-blown hurricane of love and passion whipping through a life together (getting Schwifty). We have come so far from acquaintances to friends, lovers to partners and soon to be husband and wife. Our journey has been well traveled with many adventures but merely just beginning. I look forward to adding to this story, line by line, chapter by chapter. Every laugh, kiss, smile, every riddle sent to me via chat and milestone will be cherished as much as that first moment when I handed her that creamer and said, "Hello." Until now very soon we will go from saying, "Hello" to saying, "I do."

Looking back now, I know something I didn't know then: *That* was living. Not surviving. Not numbing. Not acting out some version of who I thought I was supposed to be. This was the start of building something real. From nothing. From rock bottom. The love of self came first. That brick had been laid. With the addition of my beautiful Tiana, I began building something more. A life. A future. Under the old circumstances of the man I used to be, I would not have been ready for her. That is because back then I lied to myself and others. Survival meant lying. It meant wearing masks, playing parts, saying whatever I thought would earn love or approval even if it was false. But living? Truly living means no more lies. It means being seen fully and honestly, scars and all. To obtain that, I had to become someone new. Someone whole. Tiana would not let me run and more importantly, this time, I didn't want to. I was ready for her. I deserved her. She loves me with the same ferocity. Together we've built a life, not a stage, not a game, a life.

She holds me through the tears it took to type these pages. She sees the real me and reminds me every day that

I am indeed enough. When you stop lying, you can face yourself with honesty and you can stop merely surviving. Stop just existing. You can start *living*. I know if you are reading this you have that same strength, even if it feels hidden. Even if it feels impossible. Stephen King has a quote that sums this up perfectly from *The Shawshank Redemption*.

> *Andy crawled to freedom through five hundred yards of shit smelling foulness I can't even imagine, or maybe I just don't want to. Five hundred yards... that's the length of five football fields, just shy of half a mile . . . **and came out clean on the other side.***

That's what it was like for me. My own version of crawling through that sewer pipe, five hundred yards of pain, shame, addiction, self-loathing, and regret. It wasn't quick at all. I didn't emerge clean after one moment of epiphany. It was brick by brick, piece by piece. It was falling down and getting back up, over and over again. What matters is the fact that I did come out the other side, and when I did, I wasn't the same man who went in. I was free. Not just sober, not just barely getting by, but truly free. Living, not surviving. That's the thing about healing. It isn't an event; it's a whole process. It's one brick laid perfectly, then another. It's one choice at a time, one better day at a time. It's recognizing when you've slipped back into old patterns and choosing to fight your way out. And for anyone reading this, believe that you can do the same. You *will* do the same.

You can crawl through your own sewer pipe and come out clean on the other side. The roses on the other side are worth it.

I say this to you because if I, a once-homeless drunk, an addict, a convicted "stalker," a man broken down mentally and physically with nothing but a garbage bag of clothes and a phone can make it through that darkness and come into the light, so can you. There is life after the lies, after the shame, after the addiction. There is love. There is peace. There is *you*, fully alive, no longer just surviving. It didn't happen overnight, but the momentum was there, now it is upward momentum. It started with survival. Then it turned into stability. Then came hope and eventually... came life. That's what I had never known before. How to really live. For years I thought surviving was living. Getting through the day. Putting on the mask. Numbing the pain. Hustling for success, for money, for validation. Trying to be "the man." Pretending to be whole when inside I was still that broken child. But life is something different. Life is when you wake up in the morning with gratitude, not dread. Life is when you walk into a room and know you are enough not because of the money you make or the image you project, but because you are. Life is when you can love someone not out of desperation or need, but out of joy and abundance. That is where my Tiana comes in. To anyone reading this, especially those of you who know this pain, just know that you are not alone.

Justice is Living Life Fully

I would later learn from a friend that there would be no wedding day for Breanne. She never got married. There would be no children of her own to raise. The coward dies a thousand deaths, and though she may have avoided prison and preserved her career as a teacher, I wonder if the weight of guilt ever caught up with her in ways that the justice system never could. Perhaps a life alone and unfulfilled was her chosen path. Or perhaps it was the quiet consequence of what she had done. Either way, I am at peace with the result.

What happened to you was not your fault. It was never your fault. It does not matter what they said. It does not matter what you told yourself or continue to tell yourself to get through it. It does not matter what they made you believe about yourself. You are not broken. You are not weak. You are not less than. You were hurt and wounded. You were left in the dark and yet here you are. Reading these words. Still standing. Still breathing. That in and of itself is a major victory. Congratulations!

For a long time, I thought my life had been stolen from me. I thought there was no future left for me, just survival. But survival is not the end of the story, it is only the beginning. You can heal. You can rise. You can become something greater than you ever imagined. It won't happen overnight. It will take time, work, patience, and more than anything, love. You are worthy of that love. You deserve peace. You deserve joy. You deserve a life where your days are not ruled by shame or fear or the ghosts of the past. There may be days when it feels impossible. There may be nights when the darkness whispers that you'll never be free. Believe me, I know, but let me tell you. If I can make it through and crawl through my own river of pain and come out on the other side, you certainly can, too. And when you do, the life that's waiting for you, the real life, the full life, will be worth it.

Brick by brick, day by day, step by step you can build that life. When you finally stand in that light, you will know that you were always enough. You always mattered. You always deserved better, and now... you get to live. This is where that chapter of my life turns its last page. Not with bitterness. Not with rage. Not even with sorrow anymore, but with clarity. With peace and hope. The boy who once stood in that courtroom, ashamed and broken, is long gone. The man who writes these words today is present and whole. Not perfect. Not without scars, but whole, and living. This journey taught me that just getting by is not enough. We must fight to live. To truly live. To laugh, love, build, give, and dream. No matter what they stole from me, they could not steal my future. They could not steal my heart. They could not stop my story; I rose above the drama and negativity. You can rise above yours. Walk forward not in darkness, but in light with your head held high, your heart open, and your soul free. That's what I did and that is what I want for you.

We are no longer surviving. We are living. We are Doscriosta.

Step Five Takeaways:

1) Survival is a basic instinct, not a way of life.

2) Pain is a part of living, feeling and being. It's ok to allow for that possibility.

3). Walls keep you in, not others out.

Actions Toward Healing:

1) Don't have a bucket list, have a "now" list and cross off achievements.

2) Travel, eat, love, and live to the best of your ability.

3) Take care of your physical self just as much as your mental self. Self-care, grooming, and cleanliness are paramount.

Conclusion

There are two types of fathers in this world. There are the ones who parent from instinct and habit, and the ones who parent with intention. I had to become the second type. There was no other choice because the truth is that when you come from trauma, when you've been broken, molded, humiliated, stripped of your worth, your instincts can betray you. They're built on pain, fear and survival, not love. I spent too long reacting instead of choosing. Drinking instead of feeling. Running instead of standing. Now here I was, a father to a beautiful little girl who looked up at me with wide, inquisitive eyes.

She didn't need the version of me who survived. She needed the man I was becoming, which meant that I had to choose what kind of father I wanted to be. That is a choice I make every single day. Intentional fatherhood starts with the simple belief that your child deserves a parent who is present, whole, and who will not pass down pain. For me, that meant facing my old habits, anger, avoidance, guilt, and shame. Leaving all of that at the door. It meant answering hard questions like, "Daddy, why do you hate yourself?" It meant acknowledging her position and responding with, "Baby, no one ever taught daddy how to love himself, but I am learning, and you are helping me."

It also meant being accountable when I failed because there would be days when the past crept in. I refused to let her carry that burden. It meant letting her see my tears and my healing, not just my strength. I wanted her to know that real love makes space for imperfection and that true strength lives in vulnerability. Intentional fatherhood meant showing up with time, not just gifts. With presence, not just money. With honesty, not excuses. With love, not shame.

I saw firsthand what happens when children grow up unprotected. I lived what happens when trusted adults fail you and when the people who should have guarded you choose to use you instead. That would not be my daughter's story. Not on my watch. So, I learned to parent in a way I had never been taught. I read. I listened. I stayed curious about her needs and about who she was and who she was becoming. I didn't just tell her I loved her. I showed her every day in ways that made her feel safe, seen, and valued. The world is full of broken fathers raising broken children. I refused to be one of them. So should you. My goal was simple. I wanted to raise a daughter who never had to recover from her father and give her the tools I never had.

To build a legacy of love, not trauma. And every day, I am still building that legacy one choice at a time.

I survived my childhood, my abuser, my addictions, my losses, but I hadn't *lived*. I hadn't truly known what it was to be loved in a way that heals rather than harms. That is what Tiana gave me and the truth is that I would not have made it this far without her. She didn't just love me, she saw the man I was and the man I could be. She saw the potential even with the broken parts I still carried. Instead of judging those pieces or trying to fix me, she simply held space for them. She met me where I was with patience, understanding, and an unwavering belief that I was worthy of love just as I am.

It wasn't easy at first and for a long time I was waiting for the other shoe to drop. Waiting to be told I wasn't enough, or too damaged. Waiting to be told or shown that I didn't deserve happiness by those voices. Breanne's voice, my ex-wife's voice, as well as my own inner critic, whispered constantly, but Tiana's voice was louder. Not in volume, but in truth. She taught me love wasn't about control, dependency, or keeping score. It was about choosing to show up, to stay present, to fight for joy, to nurture each other's dreams, to forgive, and to grow side by side. She taught me that I didn't have to be perfect to be loved. That healing wasn't a straight line. That my worth wasn't defined by my past.

That woman taught me how to laugh again. I mean, really laugh without guilt or shame attached to it. She taught me that real partnership is not about one person saving the other. It's about walking through life hand in hand with both people being stronger for having the other beside them. Most importantly, she showed me that actual living was not something to fear. It was something to embrace. With her, I didn't have to survive anymore. I could finally live. Together we built a new story. One not written in trauma and shame, but in hope and love. And through her love, I was able to become a better father. You can only give your children what you believe you are worthy of giving. Pre-Tiana, I wasn't sure I deserved to be a father. Post-Tiana, I knew I was.

Love doesn't erase the past. It lights the way forward and every single day with her, I choose forward. Surviving is one thing, healing is another, but maintaining peace is the hardest part. Peace is not a destination you arrive at one day and stay forever. It is something you must choose daily. It is something you must protect, especially when you've spent most of your life in chaos. I had to learn how to keep my peace and make it non-negotiable.

I would like to share with you some of the practices that keep me steady:

1). Boundaries - It took me a long time to understand that boundaries aren't walls to keep people out, they're lines that protect your energy and your well-being. Not everyone has earned access to your time, your heart, your space, and that's okay.

2). Honesty - I lie to no one, including myself. Lies are cracks in the foundation of peace. I've seen the damage dishonesty causes in others and in myself. I practice radical honesty with my wife, with my daughter, with friends, with the world, and it frees me.

3). Sobriety - There is no peace for me at the bottom of a bottle or in the haze of a high. Sobriety keeps me present, clear and alive. Every sober day is an act of rebellion against my past and a gift to my future.

4). Self-Reflection - Peace requires knowing yourself. To assist with that, I journal and meditate. I revisit the hardest moments when needed. Not for the purpose of wallowing, but to honor the strength it took to move forward. I remind myself that I am not what happened to me. I am what I choose to do now.

5). Physical Health - The body holds trauma. Moving the damage through with exercise and breathwork keeps me grounded. When my body is strong, my mind is steadier. When I sweat, I release what no longer serves me.

6). Joy - This one took me the longest to understand. Joy is essential. It is not selfish to laugh, dance, or feel good. I seek out joy unapologetically in things like music, food, and family moments. Joy is a reminder that life is for living, not just enduring.

7). Community - I am not an island. People need people. Ideally, safe, loving, honest people that can hold us accountable and remind us we are not alone. My circle is small but mighty, and through them, my peace expands.

A Final Word to Survivors

If you are reading this, if you've made it this far, let me tell you this:

You are not broken.

You are not crazy.

You are not what they said about you.

You are not what was done to you.

You are here and that alone is a victory.

I spent years carrying shame that was never mine to carry. I spent years pretending, performing, and barely surviving. I know what it feels like to want to give up. I know what it feels like to believe you are too far gone to ever find peace, but the truth is that you can come through it and heal. You can reclaim your life and build peace brick by brick, choice by choice, breath by breath.

It will not happen overnight. You will fall sometimes. You will doubt yourself sometimes but keep going. Find your people and tell your story. Demand your truth because the world needs you. No, the world needs the real you, the healed you, the joyful you, and you deserve that life. You deserve to be more than surviving. You deserve to thrive. Trust me, if I can do it, so can you. I see you. I believe you. Keep going.

This is not the end of my story, and I hope, if anything, this is not the end of yours, either. The pages you've read here are not meant to inspire pity. They are also not meant as an apology. They are not an admission of guilt nor a plea for sympathy. They are a testament. A testament to resilience and human ability to rebuild from destruction and desecration, from the ashes of torched childhood innocence. To take a life shaped by pain, and not just endure, but to live, love, grow, teach, and thrive. Every survivor has a voice. Every survivor has a truth. Every survivor has the right to peace. This book is my peace. It is a representation of my voice being raised proudly after too many years in silence. It is my truth. I pray it reaches you so you can find yours.

To every person still fighting and has yet to see the sunrise on their healing, please keep going. You are worthy. You are enough, and this world is a better place with you in it. Thank you for walking this road with me. I hope you can now walk your own road with a little more strength.

Onward.

— TJ

Acknowledgements

This is a story about growth, redemption, and becoming a better version of the man I once was, and I did not get here alone.

To my amazing wife, Tiana. You are the love that steadied my shaking hands and quieted the storms within me. You taught me how to live instead of just existing. You are my partner, my foundation, my peace, and my fire. I thank the universe for every moment that led me to you.

To my precious daughter, Tali. Your love cracked open the walls I built around my heart. Your light saved me. Your voice gave me strength and your tiny hand on my cheek reminded me that I was worth saving. I live today with intention and purpose because I want to be the man and father you deserve.

To my best friend, Carl. My brother in every way that matters. Your loyalty, strength, and unwavering presence has carried me through the darkest of times and the brightest of victories. You never gave up on me.

To my Bomb S.Q.U.A.D. brothers. Russell, Jason, and Damon. Together, we built something real. You gave me purpose, laughter, and family when I needed it most.

To my brothers, Adrian and Tony, and my sisters, Chontra, Anika, and Andrea. We all grew up under difficult, unforgiving circumstances but here we are. We are still standing, loving, thriving, and living as good people. I am endlessly proud of each of you and grateful to walk this path with you.

To Matthew McCarthy, whose friendship and kindness has meant more than you may ever know.

To Michael Hayes, a man who has always had my back. Your loyalty and belief in me have helped keep me standing.

To my cousin Stephanie. Thank you for always believing in me. Though your name may not appear directly in these pages, I want to thank you for your support, strength, and unwavering belief in my worth.

To Uncle Grady, Michael, Tasha, Rie, and all of the other friends and family that uplifted me along the way. Your continued support means the world to me.

To my mother. Though we came from a world of hardship and cycles that were hard to break, you did what you could with what you had. Life is complicated, and people are complicated, but we move forward with compassion and understanding.

And to you, Survivor. You are not broken nor are you alone. You can and will reclaim your life. Healing takes time, living takes intention, and peace is the greatest possibility. Keep pushing because you are worth the fight.

Fin

STOKESMEDIA LLC